Praise for *Practicing the*

"We often think that spiritual formation is following the way of Jesus and abiding 'in' him. However, the author helps us to see that spiritual formation is to live 'out' the way of Jesus who abides in us. Our ultimate goal of spiritual formation is to be more like Jesus through our spiritual exercises and practices. This practical manual of spiritual formation will help you to be a little Jesus."

**REV. JOSHUA CHOONMIN KANG,** author of *Scripture by Heart* and *Deep-Rooted in Christ,* and senior pastor, New Life Vision Church, Los Angeles, California

"Wow. A beatnik Tolstoy who makes 'overcoming temptation' seem like a potentially playful enterprise. This book is full of examples of how a community might embody faith. It's immensely practical and inspiring."

**DEBBIE BLUE,** author of *Sensual Orthodoxy* and *From Stone to Living Word,* and founding minister of House of Mercy, St. Paul, Minnesota

"Mark Scandrette has brought together a remarkable array of stories, ideas and practical exercises that will enable us all to engage our faith more holistically. I loved this book and would recommend it to anyone who is looking for a more kingdom-focused, justice-oriented approach to spiritual formation."

**CHRISTINE SINE,** author, activist and executive director of Mustard Seed Associates

"This book provides something we urgently need today: a practice-based approach to spiritual formation. It is an honest account of someone, and several someones, who actually tried to do the things Jesus taught us to do. This book is inspiring because it shows a willingness to take risks, and is honest at the same time. Focusing on practice can tend toward legalism, but Mark avoids any hint of legalism by stressing the inner character over the outer action and, as he puts it so beautifully, not merely engaging in pious practices, but 'learning to dance to God's song.' In an age when we talk more about spirituality than we practice it, this book will provide us a healthy balance. It is a much-needed approach to Christian formation for the current generation and beyond."

JAMES BRYAN SMITH, professor of theology, Friends University, and author of *The Good and Beautiful God, The Good and Beautiful Community* and *The Good and Beautiful Life*

# PRACTICING THE WAY OF JESUS

## LIFE TOGETHER IN THE KINGDOM OF LOVE

### MARK SCANDRETTE

IVP Books

An imprint of InterVarsity Press
Downers Grove, Illinois

InterVarsity Press
P.O. Box 1400, Downers Grove, IL 60515-1426
World Wide Web: www.ivpress.com
E-mail: email@ivpress.com

InterVarsity Press® is the book-publishing division of InterVarsity Christian Fellowship/USA®, a
movement of students and faculty active on campus at hundreds of universities, colleges and schools
of nursing in the United States of America, and a member movement of the International Fellowship
of Evangelical Students. For information about local and regional activities, write Public Relations
Dept., InterVarsity Christian Fellowship/USA, 6400 Schroeder Rd., P.O. Box 7895, Madison, WI
53707-7895, or visit the IVCF website at <www.intervarsity.org>.

All Scripture quotations, unless otherwise indicated, are taken from the Holy Bible, Today's New
International Version™ Copyright © 2001 by International Bible Society. All rights reserved.

While all stories in this book are true, some names and identifying information in this book have
been changed to protect the privacy of the individuals involved.

The vows on page 52 are reprinted courtesy of Ryan Sharp.

Portions of chapters seven and nine were edited by Dee Dee Risher and first appeared in Conspire
magazine, Winter 2010 and Summer 2010.

Cover design: Cindy Kiple
Interior design: Beth Hagenberg
Images: ©patrimonio designs limited/iStockphoto
Author photo credit: Noah Agape Scandrette

ISBN 978-0-8308-3634-5

Printed in the United States of America ∞

Library of Congress Cataloging-in-Publication Data

Scandrette, Mark.
  Practicing the way of Jesus: life together in the kingdom of love /
Mark A. Scandrette.
      p. cm.
  Includes bibliographical references.
  1. Christian life. 2. Church work. I. Title.
  BV4501.3.S286 2011
  248.4—dc22

                                                                    2011008127

P   18   17   16   15   14   13   12   11   10   9   8   7   6   5
Y   26   25   24   23   22   21   20   19   18   17   16   15   14

To all who have participated and collaborated in
our experiments and shared practices over the years.
This book is the fruit of our common story.


To the dedicated patrons of ReIMAGINE.
This book is the fruit of your faith and generosity.

# Contents

# Part One
# Perspectives

# 1

# An Invitation to Experiment

*Therefore everyone who hears these words of mine and puts them into practice*
*is like a wise man who built his house on the rock. The rain came down,*
*the streams rose, and the winds blew and beat against that house; yet it did not*
*fall, because it had its foundation on the rock. But everyone who hears these*
*words of mine and does not put them into practice is like a foolish man*
*who built his house on sand. The rain came down, the streams rose, and the*
*winds blew and beat against that house, and it fell with a great crash.*

Matthew 7:24-27

A number of years ago I invited a group of friends into an audacious experiment in which each of us would sell or give away half of our possessions and donate the profits to global poverty relief. We were inspired by what Jesus taught about true security and abundance, deciding that an experiment would be a tangible way to explore the implications for our everyday lives. Jesus once told his disciples, "Sell your possessions and give to the poor" (Luke 12:33). And when people asked the prophet John how to respond to the reality of God's kingdom he said, "Anyone who has two shirts should share with the one who has none, and anyone who has food should do the same" (Luke 3:11). We called our experiment Have2Give1.

To our surprise over thirty people signed up to participate, and together we plotted how to sell the things we owned to help the poorest people in the world. Friends traveled an hour or more each way just to be at our project meetings. We spent the next eight weeks systematically divesting of our stuff—each week collecting different items to sell, donate or recycle. One week it would be books and music, another, clothes and household items. Everyone had a list of objects in question (Can I keep my figurine collection? Should I auction off some of my jewelry? Do I really need three bicycles?). We were excited to see how the things we owned, much of which was collecting dust, could be sold to feed and help hungry people. While selling our cars, antiques and bicycles we discovered that many of the items we thought were so precious and valuable were actually nearly worthless. Some of us wondered why we kept buying things we didn't need or use, like sales-rack clothes with price tags still attached after years in the closet. One Saturday we held a garage sale and put out a sign saying that all proceeds would go toward tsunami relief in Indonesia. With the leftovers we did a swap and then donated the rest to a local thrift store.

This flurry of activity led us to ask deeper questions about our heart posture toward money, possessions and consumption. One night we decided it would be a good idea to share how much money we made and where that money was spent. We did some further investigation into what Jesus taught about God's abundance and wrestled with how his teachings offer a subversive critique of many of our commonly held beliefs and practices. We came up with a list to summarize the qualities we had explored: contentment, gratitude, simplicity, abundance, frugality, generosity and trust. We decided to make a public statement about what we were learning by having a postcard printed with the following phrase written on it:

A new way is possible

Sell your possessions and give to the poor

> For where your treasure is there your heart will be also
> Ask and you will receive
> Seek and you will find
> The secret of contentment

On the other side of the postcard was a photograph of a hand holding a coin. We glued three thousand nickels to those cards and on Black Friday morning (the day after Thanksgiving and the busiest shopping day of the year in the United States), we handed them out to passersby at Union Square, a popular shopping district in San Francisco. In the midst of people scurrying to do their gift buying and among the homeless begging for change, we shouted, "Spare change, we've got some spare change, please have some spare change!" Busy shoppers brushed past, some refusing while others asked why we were giving away money. "Because we think there is another way to live—open-handed, trusting and generous," we said.

Through Have2Give1, thousands of dollars were redistributed and we each discovered more heart simplicity and the benefits of less physical clutter. We were surprised at the depth of connection we felt with a diverse group of people we barely knew when the experiment started. Working on an intensive project seemed to produce an accelerated sense of intimacy. Rather than merely trafficking in ideas or rituals, we now had a common story to tell. For many of us, this and subsequent experiments set a chain of events in motion that continues to shape the ongoing direction of our lives. Some of us quit jobs or relocated to impoverished communities. Others have gotten out of debt, reconciled with their families, overcome addictions or discovered significant inner healing. Many of us have experienced a greater sense of identity, purpose, security and peace. There have been many firsts: sharing a meal with a homeless person, writing a poem, telling someone about a deep wound.

Doing a tangible experiment took us out of our heads and into our bodies, required us to be honest about the real struggles of our lives, and helped us learn something about the power of taking action in solidarity. Gradually we came to realize that this kind of transformation is to be expected when we allow Jesus to be our Rabbi. But what surprised us most was how eager our friends were to take action with us. It was as if they had just been waiting for someone to ask.

Have2Give1 proved to be the beginning of what would become a vibrant collective of people who take risks together to explore how to integrate the teachings of Jesus into everyday life. Each year we engage in a series of group experiments including one-day intensives, weekend retreats, four- to six-week experiments and large-scale projects. Several generations of new leaders and communities have been activated. Hundreds of people have been a part of experiments in the Bay Area, and groups in other cities across the globe have been inspired to create their own. This book is an effort to share what we have learned with a wider audience.

## The Jesus Dojo

So many of us want to live in the way of Jesus—pursuing a life that is deeply soulful, connected to our real needs, and good news to our world. Yet too often our methods of spiritual formation are individualistic, information driven or disconnected from the details of everyday life. We simply are not experiencing the kind of transformation that is the historically expected result of the Christ phenomenon. If Jesus of Nazareth demonstrated and taught a revolutionary way of love that is actually possible, alive with healing and hope, then we need a path for experiencing that revolution in the details of our daily lives. Simply put, I believe we need to recover a sense of immediacy and action in our spiritual practices. Perhaps what we need is a path for discipleship that is more like a karate studio than a college lecture hall. With this book I hope to offer a practical approach to spiritual formation that is serious about Scripture, action-focused, communal, experiential, and connected to real world challenges and opportunities.

Aside from a vision to live in God's abundance, what motivated us to initiate Have2Give1 was our frustration with the methods of spiritual formation most familiar to us. Many of us had spent years in contexts with good teaching, or been in smaller groups where important topics were discussed and we could be honest. What we were saying, by how we gathered, is that thinking, talking and knowing will lead to transformation. I had often wondered: What if, instead of talking about prayer, we actually prayed; or what if, in addition to studying about God's heart for justice, we took action to care for needs? Or what if, instead of just telling each other about our struggles, we committed to a path for change? It seemed like the missing ingredient was a context that would encourage honesty, invite us into community and move us from information into shared actions and practices.

During my formative years I spent time with philosopher and theologian Dallas Willard, who often and memorably told us that to experience the kingdom of God "a group of people should get together and simply try to do the things that Jesus instructed his disciples to do." We don't enter the kingdom of God merely by thinking about it or listening to one another talk about it. We have to experiment together with how to apply the teachings of Jesus to the details of our lives. In discussions with friends, I began to say, "It seems like what we need is a Jesus dojo—a space where we can work out the vision and teachings of Jesus together in real life." In Japanese the word *dojo* means "place of the way" and is used to describe a school or practice space for martial arts or meditation. Theoretically, a dojo could be created for any skill or discipline. You could have a knitting dojo, a cooking dojo, a karate dojo—or a Jesus dojo. The important distinction is an *active* learning environment, where participation is invited and expected.

When I first began using the term "Jesus dojo," a friend of mine sent me a small porcelain sculpture of Jesus in a karate uniform teaching a boy and a girl how to kick and punch. The sculpture was one in a series of kitschy Jesus sports statues sold by a religious gift company that also included depictions of Jesus teaching children how to do ballet, ski, play hockey and golf. The gift was meant to be a joke, but I kept it, despite its overly literal and culture-commodifying associations, because it reminded me that Jesus taught his disciples in an embodied way that challenges our Western notions about didactic classroom learning. You can't learn karate just by watching, and we can't learn to follow Jesus without practicing to do what he did and taught. Jesus didn't just communicate information or ideas, but declared, "I am the way" and invited his disciples into a new life that was fueled and inspired by his example, teachings and sacrifice (John 14:6). As a rabbi, he taught his disciples, or *talmidim,* by inviting them to make dramatic changes in their lives—to risk new ways of being and doing. Through surrender and practice, Jesus expected his apprentices to become like him (Luke 6:40). In fact, the earliest disciples of Jesus consistently identified themselves as "followers of the Way" (Acts 24:14), suggesting that they viewed apprenticeship to Jesus as a way of life, the combination of right belief and right living—or what we might call orthopraxy. So a Jesus dojo is a space where a group of people wrestles with how to apply the teachings of Jesus to everyday life through shared actions and practices.

To offer a more precise description, a Jesus dojo, or community of practice, is (1) an experiment, (2) inspired by the life and teachings of Jesus, (3) in which a group of people commit time and energy to a set of practices, (4) in conversation with real needs in our society and within themselves, (5) and reflect on how these experiences can shape the ongoing rhythms of life. Most of us have had transformational encounters that reflect the essence of what I am describing here. The intent of this book is to help readers become more mindful of this process and more intentional about creating spaces with greater transformational potency.

I use the term "community of practice" here to describe the ancient and enduring historical phenomenon of whole-person apprenticeship to Jesus. It is the way that disciples to Jesus have always been made. When Jesus proclaimed the immediacy of God's kingdom, he asked for a whole-person response: "Repent and believe the good news" (Mark 1:15). Eugene Peterson's dynamic paraphrase highlights this text as a call to action: "Time's up! God's kingdom is here. Change your life and believe the Message." In other words, dream up your whole life again—because there is a new way to be human. Those who first heard his message began making dramatic changes in their lives based on his instructions. For example, after Jesus had taught his disciples to sell their possessions and give to the poor (Luke 12:33) we later find them doing just that: "Selling their possessions and goods, they gave to anyone [who] had need" (Acts 2:45 NIV). Together they created a shared culture—a community of practice where whole-life transformation was expected and supported.

Jesus taught with unique authority, convinced that his teachings corresponded directly to the reality of the way life actually works. He embodied and presented not a theoretical construct, but a path for becoming fully human and awake to our Creator. Like a produce vendor offering free samples at the farmer's market, Jesus seemed to take a "try before you buy" approach. He invited those who were skeptical about the divine origins of his message to test the authenticity of his teaching through experiments in obedience—confident that the truth of what he taught could be proven by experience: "Anyone who chooses to do the will of God will find out whether my teaching comes from God or whether I speak on my own" (John 7:17). The way of Jesus can be verified by direct experience and must be practiced to be understood. Through shared practices of obedience we can know the truth of what Jesus taught about the reality of God's kingdom. In the well-known parable of the wise and foolish builders, Jesus makes the point clear that putting the teachings into practice is not merely an option—it is the difference between safety and destruction (Matthew 7:24-27).

## Why We Need Spaces of Practice and Experimentation

Twenty years ago, when I was in college, the most ardent Jesus seekers of my generation wanted to become pastors, teaching missionaries or evangelistic campus workers. While we asked how we could help people believe in Jesus and prepare to die, today's college students are more likely to ask, "How can I be like Jesus and change the world?" I regularly hear the young people I meet or work with express their passion for God more holistically:

"I want to work with AIDS orphans in Africa."
"I want to live in an intentional community."
"I want to become a legal defense lawyer to help fight human trafficking."
"I want to be a community organizer in the inner city."
"I want to make films, paint pictures and write stories."
"I want to plant a garden and live more simply."
"I want to be aware of God's presence in every moment."
"I want to start an ethically responsible technology company."

The boundaries for our understanding of what it means to seek the kingdom of God "on earth as it is in heaven" are radically and necessarily expanding. This shift is not isolated to younger people. People of all ages and cultural backgrounds are sensing a pull toward a spirituality that is more holistic, integrative and socially engaged. In recent years increasing numbers of people have mentally "checked out" or physically left the Christian groups they have been part of because they have felt that these contexts are not actually helping them believe, belong or live better. While it may be tempting or convenient to blame church leaders or structures for this, I believe this widespread dissatisfaction is a symptom of the larger challenges we face as a society. Advances in technology, the explosion of information and increasing mobility have created a sense of disequilibrium and social fragmentation. The church, along with every other social institution, is grappling with how to thrive in a rapidly changing, always connected mobile and global culture.

As a result of these shifts, a new consciousness is emerging—a way of seeing the world and ourselves that is more holistic, integrative and ecological. This explains, for instance, why someone might make a connection between loving God and, in light of global inequities, adopting a simpler, local diet or lifestyle. We are becoming increasingly aware of how the body, mind and spirit are interrelated and how our individual choices contribute to the health and suffering of others, including future generations and the earth itself. In this consciousness, sin is not only an individual problem but also manifests in the brokenness we see in every dimension of life— from broken relationships to broken economies to broken water supply systems. By "ecological" I mean not only an awareness of our interdependence with the natural world, but a more basic way of seeing that appreciates and yearns for wholeness, restoration and salvation to come to every part of creation. Our increasing integrative perspective makes us groan all the more loudly for the holistic redemption that is promised (Romans 8:22). We yearn for the time when we can say, "The kingdom of the world has become the kingdom of our Lord and of his Messiah" (Revelation 11:15).

Changes in our society and consciousness are raising new questions about what it means to be faithful to the way of Jesus, and how to understand the unfolding story of the Judeo-Christian

Scriptures. We bring new questions to ancient traditions and texts. Instead of primarily asking, "How do I get to heaven when I die?" more of us wonder, "What does it look like to live conscious of God and God's purposes in the present moment?" We are rediscovering the holistic and integrative nature of the gospel of Jesus as "the good news of the kingdom" (Luke 16:16). Jesus continually spoke of a kingdom, characterized by love, that is both present and progressing. He invited his followers to "seek the kingdom" and pray that the kingdom would become "on earth as it is in heaven." He invites us into a way of life in the kingdom in which we are empowered to live without worry, fear or lust; to love our enemies and reconcile with one another; to live in generosity and trust and to instinctively care for those who are hungry, thirsty, sick, naked and lonely.

A shifting consciousness also raises new questions about evangelism and Christian witness. In a holistically-oriented culture, skeptical people are less convinced by purely rational arguments about why Christianity is true, and more curious to see whether Christian belief and practice actually make a positive difference in the character of a person's life. Knowing the transformational promise of the gospel, it is fair to ask whether a person who claims to have a relationship with Jesus exhibits more peace and less stress, handles crisis with more grace, experiences less fear and anxiety, manifests more joy, is overcoming anger and their addictions or compulsions, enjoys more fulfilling relationships, exercises more compassion, lives more consciously or loves more boldly. In any culture, but especially in one that yearns for holistic integration, the most compelling argument for the validity of Christian faith is a community that practices the way of Jesus by seeking a life together in the kingdom of love (John 13:35).

And yet, a tremendous gap exists in our society between the way of radical love embodied and taught by Jesus and the reputation and experience of the average Christian. We simply aren't experiencing the kind of whole-person transformation that we instinctively long for (and that a watching world expects to see). This suggests the need for a renewed understanding of the gospel and more effective approaches to discipleship. Though our understanding of the gospel is becoming more holistic, our most prevalent formation practices don't fully account for this. We can be frustrated by this gap and become critics, or be inspired by a larger vision of the kingdom and get creative. I believe what is needed, particularly in this transitional era, are communities of experimentation—creative spaces where we have permission to ask questions and take risks together to practice the Way.

## Renewing Our Perspective on Jesus

Shortly after we began our first series of group experiments, I participated in a large national gathering of church leaders. During a break in one of the sessions, an older gentleman introduced himself and asked, "What do you do?"

"I help people live out the teachings of Jesus," I replied.

Puzzled, he asked, "Does your work have anything to do with Christianity?"

Taken aback, my first thought was, why would I be at a national pastor's convention if I wasn't a Christian? And then I wondered, what has happened to our understanding of what it means to be Christian if helping people live out the teachings of Jesus is considered suspect?

This sincere pastor and I had stumbled into a historical argument that divides Jesus into being either a wise rabbi or a messianic savior. Was Jesus a wise teacher to admire and imitate, or a savior to believe in and worship—or both?

In the academy and popular culture, these two simplified views of Jesus are often pitted against each another. In one Jesus is seen as an exceptionally wise rabbi known for his ethics and compassion, while miraculous events, his resurrection and messianic claims are either minimized or dismissed. From the opposing view, Jesus is presented as the Savior whose death and resurrection provide forgiveness and the hope of eternal life, while his role as a model and teacher are often discounted or eclipsed by the importance placed on belief in his atoning sacrifice. Our goal here isn't to resolve a long-standing historical tension, but to ask how we can best live into a holistic understanding of Jesus that allows for the greatest transformation in our lives for the good of the world.

Our ability to practice the way of Jesus is shaped by our understanding of who he is and what his message and work mean for our lives. It is clear that Jesus intended for his disciples and later followers to actually do the things he did and taught (John 14:23-24). But as Rabbi, Jesus asks us to do what seems humanly impossible: love your enemies; turn the other cheek; forgive continually; live without lust, greed or jealousy; love as he has loved us; and "be perfect." Anyone who tries to obey these instructions quickly discovers that putting the teachings of Jesus into practice is difficult, if not impossible, without a source of power and love greater than our own. Our efforts, and subsequent failures, bring us to the point of recognizing that we need inner transformation to see a lasting change in our world.

I'm encouraged by the many signs that we are learning to appreciate Jesus both as Rabbi and Messiah, since recognizing the significance of Jesus as a savior and teacher are equally important to practicing the Way. Through his death and resurrection, Jesus makes it possible for us to enter the kingdom of love. And through his example and instructions, he teaches us how to live in the kingdom of love, sourcing our life from God's life. The earliest disciples of Jesus valued these dimensions equally, proclaiming the reality of the kingdom of God and teaching about Jesus as resurrected Messiah (Acts 28:31). The apostle Paul makes this connection clear where he writes, "[God] has rescued us from the dominion of darkness and brought us into the kingdom of the Son he loves, in whom we have redemption, the forgiveness of sins" (Colossians 1:13-14).

For the early church, the way of Jesus was a revolutionary and countercultural force, offering an alternative to the solutions and power structures of the Roman Empire. As the way of Jesus gradually developed into the religion called Christianity, it became defined more by its ecclesial rituals, doctrines and authority structures than as a grassroots movement characterized by love. After Christianity was legalized under Constantine, prophetic/monastic groups formed that continued to present the Way as a compelling alternative to the empire. When Christianity becomes the civic or folk religion of a society, fringe movements inevitably arise to call people toward more authentic and embodied discipleship to Jesus. Through the actions of smaller, more radical communities (like the desert fathers and mothers, the early Franciscans, the Anabaptists, or the early Methodists and their class meetings), the church as a whole is renewed and called forward into the redemptive purposes of the Creator. We can be inspired by those who have gone before us to discover how to practice the way of Jesus in our time and place, seeking a life together in the kingdom of love.

## An Invitation to Discovery

The premise of this book is quite simple: "Let's practice the way of Jesus." But what is simple isn't easily applied to complicated lives. We might ask ourselves why something so obvious as learning to do the things Jesus did and taught is so rarely practiced when it is something that so many of us deeply profess to desire. What excites me most about the truths explored in this book is the potential they carry to renew our experience of Christ-empowered transformation, community life and social change. My hope is that after reading this book you feel inspired and equipped to develop your own experiments in practicing the way of Jesus.

The book is divided into two sections. Part one offers a perspective on action-based group practices and details about how to begin your own experiments. Part two provides an orientation to the major categories in the teachings of Jesus and stories and samples of specific experiments and practices. I strongly encourage the reader to explore this material and try out practices together with at least one other person. Discussion questions and sample experiments are included at the end of each chapter. A suggested six-session study guide is included for use by groups.

With this book I hope to contribute to an ongoing public conversation about how we can pursue practicing the way of Jesus in the details of our lives. I trust that the examples and approach to formation communicated in these pages will seed an amazing variety of stories of transformation that far surpass anything contained here. My dream is to see communities of practice activated in towns and cities across the globe. You can visit Jesusdojo.com to contribute stories of your own experiences and see what others are doing to make a life together in the kingdom of love.

## Discussion

- *Practicing the Way.* As you think about your spiritual journey, what experiences have most helped you integrate the teaching of Jesus into your everyday life?

- *Shared practices.* When have you experienced what is being described as a community of practice? What was it like, and how have those experiences shaped you?

- *Shifts.* Where have you noticed a "shift in consciousness" in society or within yourself? How do you think this changing landscape is affecting your journey with God?

- *Stuck?* Can you relate to a sense of being frustrated or "stuck" in your spiritual practices? Where do you most long for transformation: (1) within yourself, (2) in the place where you live or (3) with issues facing our world?

- *Rabbi and Messiah.* Are you more comfortable or familiar with seeing Jesus as Messiah or Rabbi? How would you explain the connection between Jesus as a teacher to follow and a Savior to believe in?

- *Examples.* What historical figures or contemporary groups most inspire you by how they have sought to practice the way of Jesus?

- *Conspicuous absence.* Why do you think something so simple and obvious as learning to do the things that Jesus did and taught is so rarely practiced?

- *The invitation to risk and experiment.* Does the thought of a more radical, action-oriented and embodied path for discipleship to Jesus excite you or scare you? Why?

## Exercise

- *Dream up your whole life again.* Most of us, to some degree, long for something more or different in our lives that expresses our yearning for life in the kingdom of love. Sometimes the first step to getting unstuck is learning to dream again. Have a brainstorming conversation with one or two other people about what you long for and the points of resistance that keep you from experiencing life in God's kingdom more fully.

# 2

# Following the Way of the Rabbi

When I first discovered the way of Jesus, I remember how eager I was to take steps to live into my new understanding of life in the kingdom of love. As I studied what Jesus did and taught, it wasn't long before I wanted to live his kind of life. I did what spoke most immediately to me or seemed most obvious. I went through my closets and gave away any extra clothes I had. I went out of my way to make friends with people on the margins. Noticing that Jesus often prayed in lonely places, I began taking long walks alone. As an attempt to renew the "eye" of my mind, for a period of time I swore off music, movies and television. After reading "[if] your brother or sister has something against you . . . go and be reconciled" (Matthew 5:23-24), I quickly made a list of anyone I could think of that I had wronged, and started making phone calls. Trying to be a good Samaritan, I made a vow to stop and help anyone I saw stranded along the side of the road (which led to many interesting trips to auto-parts stores with strangers). Hearing that "the Son of Man has no place to lay his head" (Matthew 8:20), I started sleeping in my car whenever I could. And once, after reading, "If your right hand causes you to sin, cut it off" (Matthew 5:30 NIV), I actually took out a knife and contemplated using it.

Looking back, some of my early experiments now seem childish, sentimental or naive. But at the time they helped me get momentum in discovering how to practice the Way. And perhaps being child-like and imaginative isn't such a bad thing. Jesus once said, "Unless you change and become like little children, you will never enter the kingdom" (Matthew 18:3). The pressure we feel to be respectable or sophisticated can rob us of the sense of playfulness required to experience life in the kingdom of love. It is those little steps of obedience that propel us toward greater understanding.

I credit my parents with inspiring my early attempts to practice the Way. I remember coming down the stairs early in the morning to find my dad kneeling on the living room floor at prayer, preparing for the day. He also carried a stack of note cards with Scripture verses written on them that he used to meditate during his daily commute. My mom always seemed to be on the phone listening to peoples' problems and offering help or advice. Growing up, Tuesday night at our house was soup night for us kids (with no dessert) and fasting for our parents—so that we could share our resources with children living in places where they didn't have enough to eat. After dinner my dad would often take out the Bible, read a portion of the Gospels to us, and begin asking questions, like "What do you imagine it would look like for us to live as Jesus did?" Or he would push us to wrestle with a particular instruction: "Let's think of who our neighbors are. What can we do to love them?" Together we would generate a list of ideas to enact over the coming weeks: Invite neighbor Joe over for dinner. Shovel snow for the elderly couple down the block. Welcome a friend from school whose family is in crisis to spend the weekend at our house. One memorable holiday season my parents created a project to help us learn how to bless our neighbors. Over several nights we made Christmas decorations and cookies and then went door to door distributing them with an invitation to come to a holiday party. A few weeks later our home was full of neighbors, many of whom were meeting for the first time. The party really brought the neighborhood together, and I still remember the excitement of being a part of something bigger than myself.

My wife, Lisa, and I have three teenage children whom we have tried to raise with a similar sense of adventure and shared practices. They've grown up participating in our Jesus dojo experiments—both at home and with our tribe of friends.* We have eaten together with drug addicts, gone on weekend-long silent prayer retreats, written our own poems and prayers, helped prepare hospitality meals, and cared for orphans. We realize this might be different than the typical path of Christian education, but we think children are most impacted by the modeling and example of the people closest to them. We don't want to just tell them about the significance of a homeless messiah-prophet, we want them to walk in his steps. I'm convinced that one experience of embodied intentional practice can teach more than a year's worth of Sunday school lessons or well-prepared talks. Sometimes kids can recognize the truth of this more easily than adults. My son Noah once came with me when I spoke at a large retreat for college students. After observing several sessions where I taught, which included extended worship sets performed by an indie rock band, Noah turned to me and said, "Papa, I don't understand. You get up there and speak about things like listening to God or caring for victims of human trafficking—and then everyone leaves the building to do things that have nothing to do with what you talked about." Wherever possible, we need to create environments that include both good instruction and opportunities for shared action.

---

*It is sometimes challenging for families with young children to participate fully in group experiments if families aren't the primary focus. We encourage groups to create experiments that even small children can participate in whenever possible, or arrange for childcare so that people with small children can be involved. Family life and intentional parenting can also be an intensive community of practice.

My son Isaiah and I recently spent a weekend together doing an experiment that combined reflections on the life Christ, sessions of silent prayer and meal fellowship with people living on the streets. Isaiah was initially hesitant to go with me because praying in hour-long chunks didn't sound immediately appealing to an active thirteen-year-old. He also wasn't sure how comfortable he would feel spending time with people who are homeless and struggling with mental illness or addictions. Isaiah surprised himself (and me) by his ability to sit in stillness before God. When we went to the shelter for breakfast, we sat down by Eugene, a friendly older man who had been homeless for several years. After a lively conversation, Eugene invited us to go see where he lived. Isaiah's eyes brightened at the thought of an adventure. We followed Eugene as he briskly walked the mile to his encampment hidden under brush and trees within yards of the freeway. He showed us how to jump the fence leading to his house, an area of tarps and junked furniture. Eugene welcomed us as honored guests, inviting us to sit on his couch—an old van seat—and serving us sparkling lemonade. We held up our Styrofoam cups like champagne flutes and each gave a toast or said a prayer of thanks. Eugene shed a few tears, telling us how grateful he was to have us in his home. Before we left he gave Isaiah a baseball cap, and on the way back told us about the loss of his wife and his struggles with depression and alcohol. We had many more amazing father-son experiences of prayer and friendship that weekend, and were reminded that there are two places where we are sure to find God's presence in our world—in the quiet of prayer and in the faces of those who suffer.

I was in college when I first began to appreciate the power of taking steps of obedience in solidarity with others. One day after psychology class, my friend Forrest and I sat discussing the various mental disorders we were studying. It suddenly occurred to us that people living with severe mental illnesses must be very lonely. As followers of the Way, it seemed obvious that we would want to

seek to be friends with people struggling with mental illness. Forrest made a few phone calls and a week later we found ourselves
standing in front of a forlorn brick building that housed the ado-
lescent unit of a state mental hospital less than a mile from our
campus. While playing checkers and tossing the football we got to
know students who had killed their parents, been severely abused
or abandoned. One young man, convinced that he was possessed
by demons, pleaded with me to pray for him. I was way out of my
comfort zone and had to quickly adapt. As I listened to their stories I felt a depth of love welling up inside of me that I didn't know
I had. After that first visit I drove away from the hospital with
tears in my eyes, feeling more alive than ever before.

Some may bristle at my use of the term *experiments* to describe
practical acts of obedience like this. It's helpful to remember that
obedience to Jesus is creative—it is not just about what we won't
do, but also what we will do to be alive to the kingdom of love.
Naming these steps of obedience *experiments* acknowledges the
fact that we are in the process of finding out "what pleases the
Lord" (Ephesians 5:10). It is one thing to consider what a person
should do or might do in theory, but quite another to discern what
I will do in the immediacy of this moment. Action is the way that
we make our vision and desire for the good and beautiful tangible
(1 John 3:18). Listening to the voice of the Spirit, we take risks to
improvise new steps of obedience, not knowing exactly which actions or practices will be most helpful. A practice that is effective
for one person might not be for another. For example, extended
silence and solitude might be deeply enlightening for an extrovert,
but taking a risk to engage with people might impact an introvert
more. Also, a practice that helped us at one stage of life may not in
another. Practices are a means toward an end, not the end in themselves. So we are invited to be playful, experimenting by trial and
error to discover what actions help us become most awake to God
and empowered to love.

## Levels and Kinds of Experiments

Like me, you probably have many stories about small risks of obedience that have shaped your journey with God. As I've already mentioned, taking risks to practice the teachings of Jesus is the way that disciples of Jesus have always been made. The goal of this book is to highlight how we can be more conscious and intentional about this process and share the journey with others. As you think about the experiences and practices that have shaped you, it is likely that you have been impacted by a combination of one-time experiences, short-term projects and long-term relationships and disciplines. It's also likely that you've shared this journey with a revolving cast of characters including casual acquaintances, family members and lifelong friends. The experiments and practices explored in this book reflect various levels of relationship and lengths of commitment.

*The person-centered experiment.* The most basic experiment is person-centered. You identify a next step you wish to take and invite one or more people to join you. This is what my friend Forrest did with me by inviting me along to the mental hospital. It is the quickest and simplest way to start. Think of Jesus inviting Peter, James and John up to the mountain to pray. Person-centered experiments allow you to respond quickly to a vision or idea you have—and you can design your experiments around very specific needs or questions. For example, my friend Darren and I both wanted to be more disciplined about spending time with God but had a hard time fitting prayer into our busy schedules. We agreed to meet every Friday morning at 7:00 a.m. on a specific corner and walk to the top of a hill together in silence. Knowing that Darren would be there waiting for me often gave me the motivation to get up and pray that I would not have had by myself.

A friend can help you take a step of obedience that might seem too scary or difficult on your own. Dani realized that, among the many anxieties she struggled with, her paralyzing fear of flying was sabotaging her ability to live in the freedom of the Maker's care. She asked her friend Lauren to help her take steps to face her fear, including praying together and going with her to the airport to watch planes safely land on the runway. Gradually, Dani learned to, in her words, "Let go and give control to God," and she now flies regularly without fear.

*The group-initiated experiment.* A second kind of experiment is group-initiated. You and a few friends go through a process of identifying a felt need or concern and develop a shared action or practice. You might consider this akin to Jesus inviting the twelve disciples into his redemptive enterprise. This might be like a group of friends in their early twenties sharing practices that help them explore how to seek the kingdom of God in their careers, or parents with young children meeting to explore family spiritual practices. A group-initiated experiment requires more discussion, collaboration and leadership because you are seeking participation from a larger circle.

A group-initiated experiment can help a family or household develop a more energized life together. Trish and Win negotiated with their kids to take a thirty-day fast from media as a family. Television, the Internet, gaming systems and personal devices seemed to have taken over their lives, and they wanted to see if a fast would help them renew space for God and rediscover intimacy as a family. Trish said, "Win literally cried when he called the cable company to suspend our channel package." Reflecting on their experiment, Win said, "At first the kids weren't happy without their earbuds and video games to distract them, but gradually we all learned to enjoy spending more time together playing games or going for walks. I think we had more conflict than usual because we weren't avoiding one another by being hooked up to our machines. We had to work on resolving our issues." In the month of their media fast, Trish and Win reconnected as a couple, renewed their devotional practices as a family and had several significant talks with their sixteen-year-old son.

*The open-invitation project.* An open-invitation project is a more sophisticated kind of experiment in which a team of people collaborates to develop a project or shared practice and invites a broader network to participate. This might be like Jesus organizing and sending out the seventy-two. Knowing that a billion people on our planet live on two dollars a day or less, the leaders of a church invited their congregation to eat on two dollars a day for two weeks, collecting the money saved on food to help build wells for villages in Africa. This project helped a larger group of people do something tangible to wrestle with inequities and develop a more global economic perspective. An open-invitation project is a tangible way you can make a public offer to "practice and teach" the way of Jesus (Matthew 5:19) and introduce action-based spiritual practices to a broader community. Because it is usually offered publicly, it requires more advanced planning, a team of facilitators, facilities, and possibly a budget for staffing and expenses.

Here's an example of an open-invitation experiment in a different context. I once cofacilitated a class on spiritual practices at a large church in an affluent suburb. Each week we identified one or two tangible experiments that could be done by a large group of parents and suburban professionals with limited time. One week we challenged each other to observe a more intentional Sabbath. Another week we asked participants to shop differently—either by buying local and fair trade or by shopping for their groceries in stores where the poorest people in their city make their purchases. Another week we challenged each other to cross class boundaries by walking or taking public transportation instead of driving. The next week many people had blisters to show and stories to tell about what they learned and who they met by changing their travel patterns for one day. It was encouraging to see the shifts people were able to make by committing to just a few small steps.

Most open-invitation experiments I've helped create that are included in this book began as smaller person-centered or group-initiated experiments that proved helpful. This gave us the confidence and credibility to offer them to a larger constituency.

*The one-time experiment.* Experiments can vary in length and level of intensity. A one-time experiment is a great way to quickly begin exploring a new practice. This can be done through an evening workshop, daylong exercise, weekend retreat or weeklong intensive. It may be the easiest kind of experiment to invite someone into because it requires the briefest commitment. One-time experiments like a serving trip or solitude retreat can have a powerful transforming effect and can incubate ongoing shared practices and community life.

*The short-term experiment.* A short-term experiment happens through multiple sessions over several weeks. The benefits of many practices only reveal themselves when done consistently over several weeks or months. Having an extended yet fixed amount of time allows for more intensity, focus and intimacy. We've found that a four- to six-week commitment is a challenging but realistic time frame for most people.

*The long-term experiment.* A long-term experiment is an extended project or shared practice that a group of people commits to over several months, a year or multiple years. Usually these come from the best practices of shorter-range experiments and become the shared rhythms of an ongoing community. For example, we invite people who have done short-term experiments together into what we call tribes, a neighborhood group where people commit to a yearlong experiment in following the way of Jesus as part of an intentional community that gathers weekly. Some monastic groups and intentional communities even make lifelong commitments to journey and practice together in a particular place.

Experiments can have the feel of an encounter group, workshop, project or shared private discipline. It all depends on which mode is best for the dimension of the life and teachings of Jesus being explored. I often refer to experiments as "learning laboratories" or "learning labs" to emphasize that we are seeking to create a space where knowledge and wisdom are applied to life. A full-faceted journey for practicing the way of Jesus will involve experiments on multiple levels. You might have a practice you share with just one other person, participate in a group-initiated experiment and also initiate another practice that is more public in nature. We've found that shared experiments can be contagious. Once someone has experienced their potency they often start initiating their own. The goal is creating a participatory culture where transformation and growth are encouraged and supported.

## Rest for the Weary

After being introduced to the possibilities of a more participatory approach to discipleship, I've noticed that people sometimes react with negative feelings or guilt, wondering, "Do I really have to make such radical changes?" Or they think that a more radical path of obedience has to look like a certain kind of ascetic activist or holy person. Others wonder how they would take further steps in the midst of an already hurried life and busy schedule. For others, the potential is simply overwhelming: If the Creator's redemptive purposes are holistic, and everything matters, then where do we even start?

If the invitation from Jesus to practice the Way sounds like a burden or obligation, then we aren't hearing him correctly. The offer of the Rabbi promises the freedom we long for: "Come to me, all you who are weary and burdened, and I will give you rest. Take my yoke upon you and learn from me, for I am gentle and humble in heart, and you will find rest for your souls. For my yoke is easy and my burden is light" (Matthew 11:28-30). I love the way Eugene

Peterson paraphrases this invitation: "Learn the unforced rhythms of grace." The invitation to follow the way of Jesus doesn't help us cope with the busy lives we have or support our quest for the American dream. It does offer us a radical alternative to the ways of this world that are making us hurried, weary and tired. We are being invited to discover a way of life, in surrender to the Master, that is more fulfilling and free than any way that we could imagine or make for ourselves. All we have to do, and all we can do, is take our next step into the kingdom of love—not comparing ourselves with anyone else, but listening to the voice of the teacher showing us how to begin.

## Being God's Shalom

*Blessed are the peacemakers, for they will be called children of God.*
Matthew 5:9

Anyone we admire for the Christlike beauty of their lives became that person through a series of small steps of risk and surrender. When I first met Nate he had recently returned from a trip to Israel, where he had wandered the hills of Galilee in search of a fuller understanding of what it might have been like to be a follower of the Rabbi in the first century. Nate and his wife, Andrea, come from a world familiar with large worship services and church budgets, men's and women's Bible studies, and safe affluent neighborhoods. Yet their growing awareness of what it might mean to really seek God's kingdom "on earth as it is in heaven" had begun to pull them beyond the boundaries they knew. Nate and I read through the Gospels together, noting all that Jesus taught his disciples to do. Every week of our Have2Give1 experiment, Nate and Andrea hosted a collection of friends at their house to plot out ways to give away half of their possessions. Curious friends (who weren't even part of the project) began dropping off items to donate.

With new eyes to see, Nate and Andrea discovered a world of need in their own backyard. Day-laborers and homeless people gathered in a park less than a mile from their house and they organized a group to share meals there with them on Sunday afternoons. They befriended an older homeless woman, entering into the profound struggles in her life, and eventually invited her to live with them for a time. Their home became a place of laughter and hospitality as they learned to care for this woman, for a young couple going through a difficult time, and other friends in crisis. I'll never forget the time that a man was telling Nate and me about his methamphetamine addiction. Nate listened with such deep care and attentiveness that he didn't even notice a dog that came up and urinated all over his shoes.

As a result of their small steps of obedience, Nate and Andrea quickly became people who could invite others to take risks. They organized a neighborhood safety campaign, a graffiti-removal project and weekly meals with homeless neighbors, while balancing the needs of three small children and a mortgage. A rhythm of Sabbath days, silent retreats and getaways with friends offered a stability that allowed them to develop consistency over time. The series of projects and experiments we instigated together surfaced a network of like-minded people who have become lifelong friends and collaborators.

Nate and Andrea met Damon and Alice through Have2Give1, and discovered they had similar desires to integrate the teachings of Jesus into a shared way of life. As a new convert to Christianity, Damon quickly became disillusioned by the gap between the promise of the gospel and the passivity he observed in the church gatherings he attended. His assessment was that the church has become largely captive to the culture rather than a transforming force in society. He and Alice soon became part of the fledgling community that was developing around our experiments.

After several years and many shared experiments, Damon and Alice, together with Nate and Andrea and their children, moved into an impoverished and violence-riddled neighborhood in east Oakland where they have started a new community called Shalom and have begun to initiate experiments of their own. They worked together to fix up an old house and learned the needs of their neighborhood. Alice has planted a beautiful garden in an abandoned lot, and Damon helps neighborhood kids fix their bikes. Nate quit his old job and has started a community center with a tutoring program for kids and mentoring for at-risk youth. Andrea, who was initially hesitant to venture out from the security of their safe life, has come alive, making their home into a place of welcome for women and children in a neighborhood plagued by violence and generational poverty. Most people who knew Andrea five years ago would never have imagined how a once timid, suburban mom could transform into such a strong, courageous and compassionate woman with an ever-growing capacity to love others. And the story of where following the Rabbi will take them has only just begun.

## Discussion

- *Early steps.* Think back to the first steps you took to practice the way of Jesus. Do they now seem embarrassing or precious? Why?

- *Your mentors.* Who are the people over your lifetime who have modeled the way of Jesus for you and invited you into risks of obedience?

- *Experiments.* Are you comfortable calling acts of obedience experiments? Why or why not? What else might you call them? Why?

- *A means to an end.* Reflect on some practices that were deeply formational at one point but were less effective at another stage of life. What changed for you? How did you adapt to the change?

- *Initiating.* Think of a time when you've invited someone else into a simple shared experiment or practice. How did they react? How did their participation (or their unwillingness to participate) affect your experience?

- *The promise of rest.* How does the possibility of a more intentional and action-oriented path for discipleship make you feel? Guilty? Obligated? Excited? Overwhelmed? Explain.

- *"Take my yoke."* What do you think are your next steps to trusting Jesus more completely as your Rabbi?

## Exercise

Where does Jesus' promise of rest and freedom connect with the weariness in your life? *Meditate on the following Scripture passage* and spend some time journaling your responses to the questions that follow.

> Come to me, all you who are weary and burdened, and I will give you rest. Take my yoke upon you and learn from me, for I am gentle and humble in heart, and you will find rest for your souls. For my yoke is easy and my burden is light. (Matthew 11:28-30)

- What makes me feel weary?
- How am I burdened?
- What in my life feels heavy?
- Where do I most long for rest?
- What do I want the Rabbi to teach me?

# 3

# Creating Space
# for Shared Practices

Unless you are the queen of England, you probably don't live in a museum. We might visit a museum occasionally or, for many of us, just once or twice in a lifetime. Museums preserve the history of a nation or civilization, displaying the best achievements of artists and artisans over decades, centuries or millenniums. I've always been fascinated by the contrast between the order and prestige of museums—where works of art are displayed in rooms gleaming with marble and stationed with security guards—and the places where most artwork is made: in dingy warehouses in low-rent districts, in studios splattered with paint or piled with debris. The most important visitor to the museum is not the patron or connoisseur, but the artist, in her paint-splattered pants, who comes to the museum to pay respect and be inspired by those who have gone before her. The museum preserves the long conversation about what art is, and the community of artists labor with the hope of making their contribution to this ongoing dialogue, that one day their work will be worthy of display.

For seekers of the Way, the buildings, rituals, documents and theologies of the Christian tradition serve as a rich museum that inspires our efforts to practice the way of Jesus. They remind us that we are part of an unfolding story and an ongoing conversation about what it means to live as "children of light" (John 12:36) in our time and place. But we don't live in museums. The place where we create our "art" isn't in the clean and well-ordered world of books, historic institutions or even public gatherings, but in the grit and messiness of daily life and in our relationships with one another. The question for us is, how will we act courageously together to make our contribution to this unfolding story?

Even if you are more of a sports fan than an art lover, the point is we were made not only to be spectators (or commentators) but champion athletes who participate in the drama of the game. In this chapter we will consider steps to the process of creating your own community of practice.

## Who Can I Collaborate With?

*Let us consider how we may spur one another on*
*toward love and good deeds.*

Hebrews 10:24

*Remember your leaders, who spoke the word of God to you.*
*Consider the outcome of their way of life and imitate their faith.*

Hebrews 13:7

After hearing about the dynamics of a community of practice, people often ask, "Where can I find people who want to do this?"— assuming that the people they know in the groups they have been a part of wouldn't be interested. While this may be true, by my observation many people aren't interested simply because they haven't been invited.

Going back to the metaphor of the museum or stadium, many of us have been conditioned to be spectators rather than participants. We might consider whether the most prevalent ways we gather are helping us become transformed for the good of the world. The kind of life-on-life practices we need can't happen exclusively in rooms with hundreds or thousands of people in them. And it won't happen if we only talk about good ideas without taking action. What we choose to do when we gather says a lot about what we value and how we believe transformation happens. A major premise of this book is that most of us need less time in the museum or stadium and more time together in the studio or gym creating and training.

What I'm suggesting is that we might need to renegotiate our contracts with one another. First, we may need to renegotiate our contract of participation—from being spectators to participants. When a person joins one of our learning labs for the first time they often go through a period of adjustment because it is an environment where they are expected to participate, encouraged to be honest, asked to make decisions and invited into action. Because participatory environments are unfamiliar to many of us, we have found it helpful to be as clear as possible about what participation looks like. We let people know what the vision and goals are ahead of time and what they will be expected to do. In the words of one of our tribe leaders, "This is a group where your participation will be noticed; you will be missed if you are absent."

Second, we may need to renegotiate our contract of community—shifting from a posture of passive consumers to committed contributors. There may have been a time when life-on-life apprenticeship happened more organically in the course of daily life—when people lived and worked in closer-knit communities. But for most of us, living in a highly mobile and fragmented society, we have to make very intentional efforts to connect and share life with one another—even in our families and households. In our society "community" is a loaded term that commonly expresses our profound desire be known and cared for. I think this is why so many of us think that what we need is more casual time together socializing and hearing each other's stories. When a group promises community as its primary goal or product, we can be quickly disappointed—because what is offered can never measure up to the picture of intimacy we can imagine. People often come to our learning labs in search of a community. We patiently explain that, though we believe a sense of belonging is important, community is not the best goal in itself—it is the byproduct of shared vision, activities, practices and commitments. The quality of relationships we want can't come from a posture and attitude that asks, "How can my needs be met?" Community can't be manufactured, nor is it instantaneous. True community develops over time, through patience, love and mutual commitment.

Third, we may need to renegotiate our contract of leadership—from service provider to practitioner or guide. Leaders need to begin to see themselves not just as hosts, caregivers or communicators, but also as initiators and coaches who invite people into acts of obedience. In the documents of the earliest disciples, a leader was someone who lived in the present reality of God's kingdom and was able to teach others, by word and deed, how to practice the Way (Hebrews 13:7). You can't lead someone to a place you've never been yourself. In a community of practice the credibility of a leader is dependent on their lived experience in practicing the commands of Jesus. This implies a shift from expecting those who lead to "give us what we want," to trusting them as master apprentices who will challenge, train and guide us in a manner similar to someone teaching you how to cook or drive or play a sport. Whenever possible we encourage people to lead collaboratively, in partnership with a team, so that even the act of initiating is a shared experiment.

People often wonder how an action- and practice-based approach to spiritual formation can be applied to an existing group. It's important to recognize that any group is formed around certain agreements or assumptions about what the group is about and what is expected of leaders and participants. It wouldn't be kind or fair to suddenly change that contract—though gradual shifts can be made that give people opportunities to practice the Way together. In an existing group, a good place to begin is by simply asking one another, "What is one thing we can each commit to do, as an experiment, between now and the next time we meet?"

Not everyone is ready to participate in shared experiments and practices, and people should be free to self-select into this dynamic. My friend Alex leads a medium-sized suburban church. When he first recognized the power of practice for spiritual formation, his first impulse was to try to get the entire congregation to "buy in." He taught about the reality of God's kingdom on Sunday mornings and challenged the whole congregation to do specific experiments he came up with. Most people either ignored his attempts or were frustrated by trying to act alone. Eventually Alex changed his approach. First, he invited a few trusted friends into a shared experiment. Then he invited the congregation to sign up for a short-term small group called Praxis that would explore shared practices. The friends he first invited to experiment became his collaborators for Praxis, and sixteen people signed up to participate. As people from the Praxis group began sharing stories of life change, the idea spread throughout the congregation, seeding a new cycle of experiments.

## What Did Jesus Do and Teach?

*Come, follow me.*

Mark 1:17

Practicing the way of Jesus requires careful attention to what he did and taught. This is what the most ardent "Jesus Way" seekers of the past have done. You can start by simply considering what teachings and examples of Christ you find most compelling. When we began our first intentional experiments, we wanted to be thorough and systematic, not haphazard about what we chose to pay attention to. A small group of us read through the Gospels with these questions in mind:

- *What did Jesus say about himself?* The Gospel writers included biographical information and statements that Jesus and others made about his identity to help us appreciate his unique authority and credibility as a messenger and embodiment of the divine being.

- *What did Jesus teach about the nature of reality?* Through parables, wise sayings, conversations and declarations, Jesus spoke from true knowledge of how life really works, calling many of our commonly held assumptions into question.

- *How did Jesus model what he taught in the way he lived?* What made Jesus a distinct and compelling Rabbi and Messiah figure is that he embodied what he taught by how he lived. In every step he revealed what love looks like.

- *What did Jesus invite his listeners to do?* On many occasions Jesus gave specific instructions about how to apply his teachings to life. A few of those instructions were to a particular person (e.g., "Bring me the donkey and her colt" [see Matthew 21:2]), but most apply to anyone who aspires to practice the Way.

The information we got by asking these four questions helped us develop clear direction for how to conceive our Have2Give1 project. We noticed Jesus saying something profound about the nature of God's reality: the divine being is a caring provider and source of abundance beyond our ability to earn, produce or spend. Events are recorded that also help us appreciate the authority of Jesus. One day Jesus told Peter to go catch a fish to pay both of their taxes, and remarkably, the fish had a coin in its mouth (Matthew 17:27). We also observed how Jesus lived. He was at times homeless, yet always at home in the world. He modeled a life of simplicity and generosity, and practiced nonattachment to material wealth. And he made provocative statements like, "Life does not consist in an abundance of possessions" (Luke 12:15). Finally, Jesus gave specific directives about how to live in the reality of God's abundance and provision: "don't be afraid," "don't worry," "sell your possessions and give to the poor," etc. The combination of what Jesus taught, how he demonstrated authority and what he specifically directed his disciples to do provides us with a full-faceted understanding of how to begin conceiving specific experiments.

Sometimes concern is raised that a practice-based approach to spiritual formation, with its emphasis on experience, might minimize the importance of Scripture. By our observations, the opposite is true. When a group seeks to take action in response to the message of Jesus, Scripture becomes more important, because the stakes are raised when you intend to act on your understanding of the text. I would even suggest that the Scriptures cannot be adequately understood apart from an honest attempt to apply them to the details of life. The Scriptures have been given to us to inspire us to be awake to the Creator's reality and purposes so that we might risk obedience. Jesus repeatedly urged his audience to listen with the intent of action: "Why do you call me, 'Lord, Lord,' and do not do what I say?" (Luke 6:46). James emphatically echoes this instruction, "Do not merely listen to the word, and so deceive yourselves. Do what it says" (James 1:22). According to the apostle Paul, the Scriptures are useful to teach and train us to live in righteousness, and to equip us for every good work (2 Timothy 3:16-17). The best goal for studying the Scriptures is not to acquire connoisseur-level knowledge or complete understanding, but to gain the faith and inspiration to respond with obedience: "The secret things belong to the LORD our God, but the things revealed belong to us and to our children forever, that we may follow all the words of this law" (Deuteronomy 29:29).

For some, paying such close attention to what Jesus taught might seem like an overly literal approach that could lead to legalism. The apostle Peter saw the teachings of Jesus as "the words of eternal life" (John 6:68). We are being invited to trust that the instructions of Jesus are based on true knowledge of the way life actually works. They are meant to liberate us from the patterns of thinking and acting that are sabotaging and destroying us and everyone around us. So rather than begrudgingly asking, "What do I have to do?" or "How far do I have to go?" a better question is, "How free and alive am I willing to be?" By making an honest attempt to obey his instructions, we are faced with the existential question of which kingdom we want to live in—the kingdom of love or the kingdoms of this world. Risking obedience reveals the true posture of our hearts, deepens our experience of God's grace and presses us to be more responsive to the transforming work of the Spirit—so that we might become the kind of people who easily obey by learning to source life from the life of the Creator (John 15:5).

## How Does the Way Relate to Our Needs?

*When he saw the crowds, he had compassion on them, because they were harassed and helpless, like sheep without a shepherd.*

Matthew 9:36

A critical question to discuss is, "How does what Jesus did and taught connect with the real circumstances of our lives and the needs of our world?" When we were designing Have2Give1 we considered the consumptive impulses, fear and worry that are so prevalent in our culture and within ourselves. We also thought about our tendencies to buy things we don't need, accumulate debt and spend our time striving to maintain a certain standard of living. Aware of the basic survival needs of a billion people living in poverty and crisis across the globe, it didn't take long for us to recognize how the teachings of Jesus subvert the ways we tend to relate to money and possessions.

The challenge at this stage of developing an experiment is to keep it simple. It is easy to get bogged down with theological speculation or social analysis. We don't want anything to distract us from the primary task of wrestling with the teachings of Jesus by risking new actions together. It is tempting to talk about the tendencies of our culture or people in general, but we have to get specific about the needs and issues in our own lives. Recently, I was in a group exploring what Jesus taught about forgiveness and judging (Matthew 7:1-5). The person facilitating the discussion made some interesting comments about the symbolic implications of the speck and sawdust metaphors Jesus used. Then our group spent a good amount of time speculating about the deeper meaning of the passage. Finally someone asked, "How do you think we can apply what Jesus is saying here to our lives?" After an awkward pause, the facilitator said, "Um, I don't know if there is any direct application." Surprised, I asked, "How many of us are harboring resentment toward someone we haven't yet forgiven?" Nearly everyone in the room raised their hand. "And how many of us are in the regular habit of judging other people?" Everyone raised their hand (including me). We were able to spend the rest of our time working through specific internal and behavioral steps we would take to forgive and stop judging.

A certain degree of self-awareness is essential in order to make the connection between what Jesus taught and how it relates to our lives. In one of our learning labs, called Experiments in Truth, we ask each other two questions in the first session: What keeps you from experiencing life in God's kingdom more fully? And what is one thing you could do in the next forty days that might change your life forever? I'm always amazed by what people share. We are honest and transparent when we are expected to be. When creating a community of practice, authenticity is not something that has to be earned; it is a value that can be modeled and practiced, even by people who are meeting for the very first time. Groups like Alcoholics Anonymous have modeled this well.

It's also important to be aware of the needs and longings of the people and place where you live, and the issues we face as a global family. What this presumes is that we see ourselves as rooted in and committed to a place—which is becoming less common in our mobile and virtual culture. My friend Paul Sparks, an advocate for living locally, often asks the rhetorical question, "Who are we rubbing shoulders with enough that we could even have a reason to forgive them seventy times seven times?" Fruitful vitality comes from integrating God's story with your story and the story of the people and place where you live. An absence of integration between these components leads to a lack of power, integrity and relevance in our efforts to practice the way of Jesus.

Every culture reflects a certain longing for the kingdom of love. Where I live in San Francisco, many people feel their need for transcendence through a longing to become more creative and artistic. So when we explore God's story (theology) we often do it through the lens of the arts, calling our experiment "Awakening Creativity." Many of us wish to simplify our lives or experience deeper relationships, so we might call an experiment "Simplify" or "Creating Community" to reflect these felt needs. When we consider following Christ's instructions about caring for the least of these, this translates into projects that address homelessness, human trafficking or neighborhood safety. We discern this by asking questions like, "Who are the outcasts, the hungry, thirsty, naked, sick and lonely in our city?" Each of us can be a student of where we live and become more conscious of how the teachings of Jesus connect, not just with our personal needs, but also with the struggles of the people and place where we live.

# What Action Can We Take Together to Practice the Way?

*Why do you call me, "Lord, Lord," and do not do what I say?*
Luke 6:46

A fourth step toward creating a community of practice is developing a tangible experiment or shared practice. Our experiments usually originate with a core group of people who pray, study and brainstorm together. We trust that the Spirit will guide us toward a concrete experiment that connects with the growth needs of our group. Some of our experiments are designed around one specific directive, like "sell your possessions and give to the poor," while others attempt to encompass several instructions that are related. In a learning lab we call Creating Community, each week we do an experiment on one of the "belonging" teachings of Jesus ("be reconciled," "forgive," "do not judge," "love your enemies," etc.). Other projects are driven by a public need or concern, such as escalating violence. After the core group has created a clear and simple proposal we invite a wider audience to participate. Through trial and error (often error) we've come to recognize several elements that make up a good experiment.

A good experiment involves new actions and changes in habits over a fixed period of time. I was once part of a group where we tried to come up with a shared practice based on the command, "Love one another. As I have loved you, so you must love one another" (John 13:34). We quickly came up with proposals like "go out of your way to be kind to someone this week"—but many of our initial ideas seemed trite and didn't get at the fact that, for Jesus, loving action was not a discrete event, but the pervasive posture of his entire life. So we pressed each other further by considering what discipline we might commit to that would push us to express love in all of our interactions with people. It took us awhile, but what we came up with was simple yet dramatic. We decided that for our experiment we would try to see as God sees. We made a commitment to consciously look into the eyes of each person we met, pausing to see them as God's beloved child and our brother or sister.

A good experiment has intensity and requires high commitment. Regular and repeated practices often have more transformational potential than an action that is only taken once. An experiment might include daily practices that are punctuated by provocative one-time actions. For example, you might commit to pray every day for your enemy, do something to bless them once a week for six weeks, and share a meal with them once during the course of a multiweek experiment. When we invite people into experiments we provide a very clear description of the project and what is expected. Vague or ambiguous experiments lead to vague or indiscernible results. We also sign a contract of participation and sometimes ask for a sliding-scale financial contribution toward any costs. In general we find that people take their commitments more seriously when they pay to participate—which creates greater expectation and openness for learning.

A good experiment provides space for both action and reflection. It's hard for most of us to adopt a new practice consistently or take a bold new step of obedience without a supportive space to process and reflect. Most of our experiments and projects (except for weekend or weeklong intensives) run from four to six weeks and usually include a weekly project meeting with a small group check-in and a large group action or practice. The consistency and accountability of a group encounter help us make changes or take risks that might be too challenging for us to do alone.

## How Can We Integrate What We Discover into the Ongoing Rhythms of Our Lives?

*Join together in following my example, brothers and sisters, and just as you have us as a model, keep your eyes on those who live as we do.*

Philippians 3:17

We started our shared experiments with a one-time project. Yet after its success, a core group formed that wanted to continue experimenting together, and that group eventually began to identify as a distinct community. Over the next year, every two months we launched a new experiment based on one core theme from the life and teachings of Jesus. At the conclusion of each experiment, we asked ourselves, "What did we learn that we want to integrate into the ongoing rhythms of our lives?" We made a list of the experiences and insights that shaped us over the previous year. Gradually we identified seven themes that became the core values of our community and the vows we take together each year.

> To Creator, obedience
> To Creation, service
> To each other, community
>> In all things, love, in all things, love
> With possessions, simplicity
> For life, prayer
> In our world, creativity
>> In all things, love, in all things, love
> —Ryan Sharp, 2007

Some of our experiments have been well designed and effective, and others have been poorly conceived or poorly executed (and frankly, quite embarrassing). We have probably learned as much through our failures as our successes. However, I am proud that we took the opportunity to try, fail, learn and try again. Some people participate in one or two experiments and move on, while others become part of the core, eventually leading experiments or starting new groups. What we hope to cultivate together is a generative space where transformation is likely to occur. There are several ways that we measure success:

- *Stories.* Are we becoming more loving and self-aware, experiencing healing and making better choices in our lives?

- *Fertility.* Are new people being invited and welcomed into our adventures? Are leaders being empowered who can initiate new experiments and groups?

- *Quality.* Was our experiment well organized, clear and easy for people to engage with? Did we accomplish what we set out to do?

- *Witness.* Does our experiment have a public face that expresses the wonder, beauty and power of God's kingdom?

- *Artifacts.* Did our experiment produce an artifact that can inspire and equip others (such as a story, poetry, artwork, songs, newspaper articles, a website or other resources)?

- *Prophetic.* Did our activity push the conversation forward, deepen the standard of apprenticeship, and provoke reaction beyond our group?

At first glance, creating space for shared practices might seem like quite a serious or ominous task. But like creating a work of art or training to play a sport, it is a task that requires both discipline and a sense of whimsy, playfulness and fun. We are being invited into the adventure of discovering what it means to be "children of light" who jump and laugh and play along the path.

## Discussion

- *Museum to studio.* Do you tend to think of the spiritual life more like a museum or an artist's studio? Why?

- *Identifying collaborators.* Who are some people in your life that you can imagine collaborating with in shared experiments?

- *Changing our contracts.* Where have you seen spiritual leadership that flows from a depth of lived experience? Does the contract you have with the faith community you are involved with make it easy or difficult to engage in shared practices? What "contracts" do you think need to be renegotiated to create space for you for shared practices? Why?

- *What Jesus did and taught.* Brainstorm as many of the instructions of Jesus as you can. Which of the teachings of Christ do you find the most compelling? The most difficult? The most inviting? How do Jesus' teachings challenge conventional notions about how life works?

- *The role of Scripture.* "The Scriptures cannot be adequately understood apart from an honest attempt to apply them to the details of life." How do you react to that statement? Do you agree or disagree? Why? How do we obey the instructions of Jesus without becoming too literal or legalistic?

- *Honesty and self-awareness.* Do you find it easy or difficult to be vulnerable with people about the real issues and needs in your life? Why? What are the ingredients that create an environment of safety and trust?

- *People and place.* How would you describe the local culture you are part of? What needs, values and longings are being expressed? Where do you sense a yearning for God's healing to come to the struggles in our world?

- *Rhythms of life.* What are some rhythms and practices you want to share with others to sustain and express your deepest values?

## Exercise

*Learning to pay attention.* Over the next week, read through the Gospel of Matthew or Luke, asking the following questions:

- What did Jesus say about himself?
- What did Jesus teach about the nature of reality?
- What did Jesus tell his listeners to do?
- How did Jesus model what he taught in the way he lived?

If you have extra time, read the Gospel of John. How does John's Gospel, which differs dramatically in style and intent from the other Gospels, complement the message of the other Gospels?

# 4

# The Vision and Physicality of Spiritual Formation

*Everyone who competes in the games goes into strict training. They do it to get a crown that will not last, but we do it to get a crown that will last forever. Therefore I do not run like someone running aimlessly; I do not fight like a boxer beating the air. No, I strike a blow to my body and make it my slave so that after I have preached to others, I myself will not be disqualified for the prize.*

1 Corinthians 9:25-27

At the party, Scott found me in the kitchen getting more cheese and bread. After telling me about his recent business trip to Morocco, he leaned forward, lowered his voice and said, "Um, so, I heard about your little 'experiment.' . . . It sounds pretty intriguing."

"Who told you?" I asked. "We were trying to keep it a secret."

"Word travels fast. I heard it's pretty intense. So, what are all the things you are giving up?"

"Well, it's not just about what we are giving up. It's an experiment—to see what difference a few changes might make. The four of us made a forty-day vow: no meat, no media, no solo sex, a limited wardrobe—and a promise to memorize the Sermon on the Mount."

Looking impressed, Scott said, "Wow! How'd you come up with all that?"

"One night we were talking about wanting to have more focus and momentum in our lives. We started reflecting on the things that distract us, take up our time, and some of the unhealthy ways we tend to deal with stress. We thought doing an experiment might help us become more awake to God and open to people. Each commitment relates to an issue that one of us struggles with—or a change we've been contemplating."

"So I understand no media and no solo sex, but why no meat?" Scott asked, while apologizing for eating a second sausage in front of me.

"We were curious about how diet relates to the rest of life. I suspect that eating meat makes me more aggressive and encourages my sense of entitlement—because producing meat uses up a disproportionate amount of the earth's resources. Most people on the planet can't eat meat as often as we're used to."

"And what have you discovered so far?"

"I feel less sluggish—although I've had to be more careful to make sure that I get enough nutrients and protein. Some of the other guys work out a lot, and they are really suffering."

"I think the 'no media' part would actually be the hardest one for me. What does that involve?"

"No television, movies or non-work-related computer or Internet use. Since we all struggle to find space to pray, meditate or care for people, we thought taking a break from media would free up space to pursue the things we really value. So far I'm spending more time with my family, doing more reading—and am getting a lot more sleep."

"I hate to think of how much time Susan and I spend watching TV—I'm pretty sure I'm addicted to the Internet. I'm curious, though, why you chose to limit your wardrobe."

"As you know, all four of us, but especially me, tend to be pretty concerned about fashion and appearance. Wow—nice boots, by the way! Where did you get them?"

Pulling up his pant leg, Scott showed me his new midcalf Italian designer boots. "Thanks. I got them on a stopover in Paris on my way home from Morocco."

After admiring Scott's boots, I returned to his question. "So anyway, we thought it would add an element of simplicity if we could wake up every morning and put on the same clothes without thinking about what to wear. At the beginning of the month we all boxed up the rest of our clothes and put them in storage. We each have two outfits and one set of workout clothes."

"And how, exactly, is this helping you?" Scott asked skeptically.

"Wearing the same thing every day reminds me I don't need more to be happy." I could see by the expression on Scott's face that this was all starting to sounding very strange. "What is it?" I asked.

"Well, it's just not what I'm used to, and frankly, it sounds a bit legalistic. My parents were part of a religious group that had a lot of rules—like no dancing, no drinking, no R-rated movies and no swimming on Sundays. I thought our generation was just getting beyond all that to experience more grace and freedom."

"I think I understand what you mean. A rule is oppressive when you impose it on others or judge them by it. But there is real power in choosing limits that add value to our lives. We are trying to be playful and lighthearted about this. I'm getting momentum in some areas where I have resisted change for a long time. And it's been easier than we thought to stick to our commitments because we are doing it together."

"So what happens at the end of the forty days? Is it back to red meat, solo sex and lots of TV?"

"Right now," I replied, "we are meeting up once a week to talk about what we are learning. We aren't obligated to stick with these practices if we don't find them helpful—though we'd all like to be less compulsive about our eating and buying habits, as well as our sexuality. So we are considering how to have better boundaries. For instance, some of us are thinking about limiting our media time to three or four hours per week, or eating meat just four times a week instead of fourteen."

Our conversation was abruptly interrupted by the sound of musicians warming up in the living room. Over the noise of the open mic, Scott spoke directly into my ear, "I don't know if I'm quite ready for that kind of intentionality. But I can see that it is working for you, and I envy the mojo and camaraderie you guys have."

## The Physicality of Spiritual Formation

Since ancient times, earnest spiritual seekers have explored ways to discipline their minds and bodies—leveraging their lives toward a greater purpose. An early advocate of the Way wrote to his apprentice, saying, "Train yourself to be godly. For physical training is of some value, but godliness has value for all things, holding promise for both the present life and the life to come" (1 Timothy 4:7-8). A discipline is an activity within our power that enables us to accomplish that which we cannot do by direct effort.* Like training for a sport or learning to play the piano, we can train to do things we could never do otherwise. Training requires a purposeful change in normal activities and patterns of habit—either an action you abstain from or a new action you engage in. Disciplines are useful for connecting and directing the mind, body and spirit toward the same goal—the undivided, love-oriented life we were created for.

One night I heard a desperate knock at the door. Greg, an irregular visitor to our community, said he needed to talk. "I'm in a real mess and I need you to pray for me," he said as we walked together in the cool night air. He went on to describe his recent

---

*Dallas Willard, *The Great Omission* (San Francisco: HarperSanFrancisco, 2006), p. 30.

sexual involvement with a woman he was casually seeing, and the anxiety and stress he felt about his mounting debts, including thousands of dollars owed to an ex-girlfriend. "Please pray that God will free me from these bad habits," he said. I hesitated, knowing that Greg tended to look for magical solutions to his persistent problems. Gently I asked about his dating and financial practices: "What are your boundaries for relating with women? Do you have a plan for how you are going to deal with your debts?" Like we've all done at times, Greg resisted facing how his choices were contributing to his present suffering. "Anything that I can do to change will take months or years—I need a solution now!" he exclaimed. Apologetically I said, "I'm not going to pray for you in the way you are asking me to—because I'm not sure that God can help you until you are willing to use the power you've already been given."

When I suggested that Greg consider how intentional disciplines and practices might help him, he had an extremely negative reaction: "That just ain't how God works." God's activity, in Greg's experience, had been "like a two-by-four upside the head"—a disorienting surprise that awakened change in his life. Rock-bottom, near-death and Damascus-road experiences are gifts, some of the many ways that God initiates transformation in our lives. But we've also been given the ability to imagine, plan and set direction, choose our objectives, and order our activities according to vision, values and goals. God is active and honored in the intentional and proactive choices we make to cooperate with the energy of the Spirit.

Of course, it would be great if we could take a tiny pink pill or pray and magically be changed, erasing the consequences of many years of our choices. But we would miss the essential truth that we were made "a little lower than the heavenly beings and crowned . . . with glory and honor," and are "rulers" over the work of God's hands (Psalm 8:5-6). We have each been given the power, authority and capacity to deliberately choose how we will live in our bodies, what we will do with our thoughts and feelings, and how we spend our time. Healing change comes as we learn to direct our life energy in new ways. If we do what we can, the Creator will do in us what we cannot. In this way, grace is not opposed to action or effort. This is why one of the early followers of Jesus wrote, "Continue to *work out your salvation* with fear and trembling, for it is God who *works in you* to will and to act in order to fulfill [God's] good purpose" (Philippians 2:12-13, my italics). We live in the now and not yet of the gospel as people in the process of "being saved" (1 Corinthians 1:18). Jesus spoke of two kingdoms in opposition to one another: the kingdom of God and the kingdom of this world—or what the apostle Paul described as the kingdom of light and the dominion of darkness (Colossians 1:12-13). We've lived much of our lives in the kingdom of darkness, having inherited and perpetuated an "empty way of life" (1 Peter 1:18).

We begin to reimagine a new way first by considering what the old and tired patterns are that need to change. Although we are now free to source our life from God's life, our bodies, minds and hearts have been conditioned to choose ways that are destructive. We are being invited to "take off" our old practices—like sexual immorality, impurity, lust, evil desires, greed, anger, rage, malice, slander, filthy language and deception—and "put on" new practices—like compassion, kindness, humility, gentleness, patience, forgiveness, love, peace and gratefulness (Colossians 3:5-17). To more fully inhabit the kingdom of love, our minds and bodies must be systematically retrained (Romans 6:13). For instance, Matthew reports that Jesus took a very pragmatic approach to helping people deal with their destructive tendencies: "If your hand or your foot causes you to stumble, cut it off and throw it away" (Matthew 18:8). Though he was using inflammatory language here, the underlying message is clear: we should do whatever is necessary to face our shadows and brokenness. Elsewhere Jesus said, "Whoever wants to be my disciple must deny themselves and take up their cross and follow me" (Mark 8:34). Endurance, discipline and suffering are realities that accompany spiritual growth and development.

Consider two examples of people who, having identified a need for change, learned to address their issues through disciplines of abstinence and engagement.

*Emily.* Emily described herself as a manically social "drama queen." She struggled with paralyzing anxiety, and when not at work, she was on the phone or out with friends talking about her worries. She was tired of being the "needy person" and wanted to live with greater trust. As an experiment, she decided to work on becoming more emotionally grounded. First she limited her social outings to one night per week. She also committed to spending a half hour each morning keeping a prayer and gratitude journal. And she asked her friends to help her become more aware of her anxious or negative comments. If they heard her say anything foreboding, they would ask her to speak five things that she was grateful for. At first, the silence and stillness of being alone were terrifying. But gradually, her prayer and journaling times helped her understand the heart issues that contributed to her emotional instability and manic tendencies. She learned to surrender her worries to God, and summoned the courage to work through other issues that surfaced with a trusted counselor.

*Kevin.* Kevin was troubled by his frequent and compulsive use of Internet pornography, but felt powerless over a cycle of guilt, depression and illicit escapes. He decided that rather than focusing solely on the behavior, he would consider other factors that supported his addiction. He realized that he used pornography when he was either bored or stressed, usually in the late evening after his family had gone to bed. He made a commitment not to open his computer after dinner, to get up early and exercise each morning, and to go to bed by 10:00 p.m. When Kevin kept these commitments, the frequency of his pornography use decreased dramatically. Early morning exercise was good stress relief and made him ready for bed by 10:00 p.m. And by limiting his access to the computer, he found more constructive and social activities to occupy his evenings. Even though Kevin felt powerless in the moment of temptation, he discovered that he had control over factors that made him less likely to be tempted in the first place.

## A Vision for Life in the Kingdom of Love

With our first group experiments, the new practices we tried took a lot of effort and required more rigor and discipline than we were used to. One of the first lessons we learned was that we weren't actually very good at keeping our promises or saying "yes" and "no" with integrity (Matthew 5:37). Sometimes we would choose an experiment just because it seemed risky, radical or extreme, without having a well-reasoned motive. At other times, adopting a new practice took so much concentration that we forgot why we had chosen the practice in the first place. Over time we learned how important it is to be mindful of a greater vision for experiments and practices.

Practicing the way of Jesus is inspired by a vision of the present availability of the kingdom of love. Jesus said that he came to bring life "to the full" (John 10:10) and described eternal life as a state of restored relationship with God we can experience now that will continue on forever (John 17:3). It is a life that finds its source and energy in God's life. We might simply say that the way of Jesus is life in the kingdom of God—or life as we were created to experience it. The two greatest commands of the ancient Scriptures give a picture of this life: to love the Creator God with our whole being (Deuteronomy 6:5) and to love our neighbor as we love ourselves (Leviticus 19:18). Or to say it another way, we were created to do justice, love mercy and walk humbly with God (Micah 6:8).

To awaken imagination and desire for life in the kingdom of God, Jesus used metaphors and stories that his listeners could relate to. He would often start his stories with, "The kingdom of God is like . . ." and then continue with "a tiny seed that grows into a great tree," or "yeast that works through a whole batch of dough," or "a lamb that got lost but has now been found." For those of us less familiar with baking and farming, we may need new pictures to help us imagine what life in the kingdom can look like. One of my favorites is that the kingdom of God is like . . . a dance.

Since the dawn of time the song of God has echoed throughout the universe. We were made to hear this song and move to the rhythm of the music, with each person's dance being unique. While most creatures instinctually dance to God's song, human beings choose whether or not to listen and respond. Gradually we stopped hearing the song, and eventually became deaf to the lyrics and melody. We found other songs to sing, with violent rhythms that made us flail and crash into one another. The original dance became a fading memory that still fills our hearts with longing. Poets and prophets were sent to remind us of the score so we could rehearse and return to the dance. Finally, a Chosen One was sent, at great cost, to heal our deafness and teach us how to move to the rhythm of God's song again. First, a few of us began to hear the music, so beautiful and alive—it made us not want to dance to our own songs anymore. Now more and more of us are entering a dance that will eventually enchant the whole world. Together we will become one great throng, hearing the same song, and moving in rhythm with the divine aria.

From bhangra to salsa, flamenco to polka, few events are as moving to me as watching people dance exuberantly to their native songs. I like the metaphor of learning to dance to God's song because it can help us appreciate that transformation is a gradual process. You awaken to the sound of the music and then slowly learn to move your body to its rhythm. For many of us, dance brings up conflicting thoughts. *Is it okay? Will I remember how? Can I risk other people seeing me try to move my body?* In our learning labs I often invite people to experience this metaphor viscerally by putting music on, turning down the lights and getting everyone up on their feet. I encourage people to feel the rhythm of the music, and then demonstrate a few simple moves—of course making a fool of myself. After some initial hesitation, people gradually become less self-conscious and begin to move their legs, arms and hips. Pretty soon the whole room is swinging to the beat of the song and we surprise ourselves by how free and expressive we can be.

Through intentional experiments and practices we learn to dance to God's song again—hearing the music and responding with movement. For practicing the way of Jesus, the vision of the kingdom is the music and the instructions of Jesus are the dance steps. The example and teachings of Jesus show us what life in the kingdom of love can look like. As my friends and I studied the Gospels, particularly the Synoptics (Matthew, Mark and Luke), we noticed there are between forty and fifty specific directives that Jesus gave about how to be a disciple (these will be explored in more detail in part two). We quickly realized that it would be difficult to track or remember so many instructions. So we began looking for "buckets" in which we could organize these teachings. The teachings of Jesus seem related to five basic themes of human experience: (1) identity (Who am I?); (2) purpose (Why am I here?); (3) security (How will I survive and thrive?); (4) community (How can I belong?); and (5) freedom and peace (What can I do about my temptations and suffering?). We noticed these themes mirrored in the apostolic letters of the New Testament and reflected in the prayer that Jesus taught his disciples, which makes them easy to remember, and suggests the possibility that Jesus may have taught his disciples to pray according to this pattern precisely because it gives a vision for the life we were made for

(Matthew 6:9-13). Here is a picture of life that we get from the instructions of Jesus:

*1. Identity: "Our Father in heaven, hallowed be your name."* Our Creator is present and caring. Who are we? We are intimately loved by a Creator who is closer than our very breath. We are not alone and we have not been abandoned. We are beloved and cared for simply because we are God's children. We don't have to earn, beg or appease God. We may have called another "Mother" or "Father," but our true parent and our real home is the eternal Abba. We were created for intimate union with our eternal parent, sourcing our life from God's life. Nothing else can ultimately satisfy us. In faith we surrender to Jesus as our Savior and Teacher, trusting that the one who made us always has our best interest in mind. This is why we are invited to live and pray the words "Our Father in heaven, hallowed be your name." An apprentice to Jesus learns to find their primary identity in communion with the triune God.

*2. Purpose: "Your kingdom come, your will be done, on earth as it is in heaven."* We were created to serve the higher purposes and healing heart of the eternal God. Why are we here? Look! All around us the Creator is at work liberating and restoring what is broken and inviting all people to return to their source. You and I were made to find our deepest joy and greatest satisfaction not from doing whatever we want, but in surrender to the Creator's desire and imagination. We are the light this world needs. We are agents of God's healing, justice and love—especially for the poor and weak and those who suffer. We don't have to be concerned about becoming the greatest or getting credit. The Father sees and knows the good work we do to serve in love. We can ask for God's reign to come to every place and person in our path and expect to see freedom multiplied. This is why we are invited to pray and live the words "Your kingdom come, your will be done, on earth as it is in heaven." An apprentice to Jesus learns to make the realization of God's creative and restoring work their highest priority.

3. *Security: "Give us today our daily bread."* God's abundance supplies everything we need. How will we survive and thrive? We are sustained through the Creator's abundance. Our Maker delights in giving us what we ask for. We don't have to be greedy because the resources we need will always be provided. We can share what we have and what we receive. We don't have to worry or be afraid of anything, including the future or what will happen to us after we die. We don't have to be jealous of people who hoard things, thinking that we live only by what we can see. Knowing where true provision comes from, we are free to live generously with content and grateful hearts. This is why we are invited to live and pray the words "Give us today our daily bread." An apprentice of Jesus learns to rely on the resources the Creator provides.

4. *Community: "Forgive us our debts, as we also have forgiven our debtors."* Access to an infinite source of love can transform our relationships with one another. How can we belong? We are infinitely loved, having received an eternal source of love to share with others. We are forgiven by God, and are empowered to forgive whenever we are wronged. Broken relationships can be restored. We can live at peace with one another. Love frees us to live without anger, bitterness, lust or judgment. We can be authentic and honest with each other and keep our promises. We can love and bless the people who take advantage of us or even hate us—because love wins over all. This is why we are invited to live and pray the words "Forgive us our debts, as we also have forgiven our debtors." An apprentice of Jesus learns to love as we are loved.

5. *Freedom and peace: "Lead us not into temptation, but deliver us from the evil one."* We can have victory over temptations and peace in suffering. What can we do about our temptations and sufferings? Be awake to God's presence and power here with us. We have the strength to overcome any obstacle. We don't have to be dominated by our feelings or impulses or the tyranny of rules and regulations. When we are weary, tired, stressed or sad we don't have to give in to

habits or compulsions that are destructive. We can overcome any temptation and endure any difficulty. Grace will meet us in the moment of our greatest weakness. We can have peace when we suffer. Nothing that happens can separate us from the eternal source of love. This is why we are invited to live and pray the words "Lead us not into temptation, but deliver us from the evil one." An apprentice of Jesus learns to practice self-denial and endure the difficulties that come from living in a divided world.

We've been invited into an amazing life through the sacrifice of Jesus and the miracle of his resurrection. Looking over this description of life in the kingdom of love it can sound almost too good to be true. Imagine a life of complete trust and contentment, a life without anger, jealousy or lust, a life where every moment is lived in response to the loving heart of God. One step toward experiencing life in the kingdom is to have a vision for what is possible and to want what is possible. It might help to even speak these intentions: "I want to taste the intimacy of being God's beloved child. I want to collaborate with God's creative and redemptive work in the world. I want to live without worry, jealousy or lust. I want to forgive and love as I have been forgiven and loved. I want to experience victory over the temptations I struggle with and feel God's peace when I suffer."

Practicing the way of Jesus begins with having an imagination for life in the kingdom of love, desiring that life, and then taking steps to live into that reality through tangible changes in how we live in our minds and bodies. We are being invited to respond to two enduring questions: What do you want? And whom do you seek?

## Discussion

- *Gaining momentum.* What thoughts, feelings or reactions surfaced as you read about the forty-day experiment introduced at the beginning of this chapter? Can you think of a time that you've taken a risk of obedience like this in solidarity with others?

- *Grace and effort.* How would you explain the relationship between God's grace through the work of Christ and the effort required to experience life in the kingdom of God?

- *The role of discipline.* Why is physical and mental discipline necessary for spiritual formation?

- *The kingdom of God.* How would you describe the vision of life in God's kingdom that inspires practicing the way of Jesus?

- *Human experience.* Discuss how the gospel of Jesus addresses these five basic questions:
  - Identity (Who am I?)
  - Purpose (Why am I here?)
  - Security (How will I survive and thrive?)
  - Community (How can I belong?)
  - Freedom and peace (What can I do about my temptations and suffering?)

- *Desire.* Experiencing life in the kingdom of love begins with vision and desire. Jesus often asked people, "What do you want me to do for you?" Take turns listening to one anothers' responses to these questions: What do you want Jesus to do for you? Where do you most desire the transformation offered through life in the kingdom of God?

## Exercise

*Pray the Lord's Prayer for another person.* If the Lord's Prayer provides a summary of the life we have been created for, praying this prayer for ourselves and for one another can be a powerful way to train and express our desires for life in the kingdom of love. Pair up with someone and pray through the phrases of the Lord's

Prayer for each other, keeping eye contact as you work to personalize the words to fit their situation. For example, "God, you are Brian's true parent. Help him embrace his identity as your beloved son, learning to be constantly aware of your presence in each moment of this day."

*Identity.* "Our Father in heaven, hallowed be your name."

*Purpose.* "Your kingdom come, your will be done, on earth as it is in heaven."

*Security.* "Give us today our daily bread."

*Community.* "Forgive us our debts, as we also have forgiven our debtors."

*Freedom and peace.* "Lead us not into temptation, but deliver us from the evil one."

# 5

# How Practice Changes Us

## The Inward/Outward Journey of Transformation

*For the kingdom of God is not a matter of talk but of power.*
1 Corinthians 4:20

The term *spiritual formation,* as it is often used, connotes the practice of solitary introspection, the reading of "classic" books on prayer or monthly visits to a spiritual director. Interest in these activities seems to increase with age and tends to focus, whether intentionally or not, primarily on the interior life of the individual. While the "inner journey" aspects of spiritual formation are obviously important, they must be held in tension with the need for an active, communal pursuit of the way of Jesus.

If there is a revolution in spiritual formation afoot, it is in our understanding of how the inward and outward aspects of discipleship to Jesus integrate with one another. "Outward journey" practices, like service, help us recognize where we need further heart transformation in order to love more courageously. Inward journey disciplines, such as prayer, when done appropriately, make us more aware of the Spirit's promptings to express love in action.

A story from the lives of the early disciples aptly illustrates how inward and outward practices interact with God's power to produce transformation. When Peter and John were on their way to the temple at the time of prayer, they saw a disabled man begging by the gate. When he asked them for money, Peter said, "Silver or gold I do not have, but . . . in the name of Jesus of Nazareth, walk." Peter pulled him to his feet and miraculously his legs were made strong. He went with them into the temple courts "walking and jumping, and praising God" (Acts 3:1-10).

The details of this story are enlightening. First, Peter and John, being devout and disciplined Jewish men, were on their way to the temple at a fixed hour to pray. Second, they went together. Third, Peter had no money—possibly because he had already given what he had away in response to Jesus' earlier instruction. And from Jesus' example, Peter had learned to pay attention to outcast people and the immediate promptings of the Spirit.

In this chapter I'd like to describe one session of an open-invitation group experiment to illustrate how inward and outward journey dynamics together can create transformation and social change.

✦   ✦   ✦

In a globally connected world, where our choices affect people on the other side of the planet, what does it mean to "love your neighbor as yourself"? That was the question that prompted a project called Abolition, a six-week experiment designed to address local and global issues of human trafficking. It is estimated that twenty-seven million people worldwide are currently affected by labor and sex slavery. Prior to the start of our experiment, a few of us spent time educating ourselves about human trafficking issues. And we met with local agency representatives to see what we could do to serve and advocate on behalf of victims. Our ambition was to help each other become compassionate and educated activists. Together we worked out a list of goals and tasks that we shared with the people we invited into our project.

1. Wrestle with the implications of what Jesus taught about love, justice and advocacy.

2. Become more educated about the issue and scale of human trafficking through reading, research and neighborhood walks.

3. Examine how our personal choices support human en-slavement—and make changes to our normal patterns of consumption to support ethical and fair-trade commerce.

4. Provide tangible care for victims of human trafficking by doing neighborhood assessment and outreach with an organization that works with survivors.

5. Practice political advocacy for victims by writing letters to local, state and federal officials.

6. Give time and financial support to organizations helping victims, and enlist the help and support of friends through an awareness and fundraising campaign.

7. Fast and pray weekly for victims of trafficking and their oppressors.

Most of us were already passionate about the issue of human trafficking. We were aware of how items we buy every day are part of the slavery supply chain. And we knew that writing letters to corporations and public officials is an important step of advocacy. But this project gave of us the solidarity, momentum and structure to act on all our good intentions.

For our Abolition project we met in Chinatown near a famous section of strip clubs and massage parlors—many of which serve as fronts for trafficking-related prostitution. You couldn't get into the building without being confronted with the desperation of people hustling, selling crack or fighting on the sidewalk. At ten after seven, Dani, a leader from one of our tribes, kindly asked us to take our seats and led us in the prayer we say together at the beginning of each session:

> Make me an agent of your healing and justice
> To weep with those who suffer
> To speak for our sisters and brothers
> Whose voices cannot be heard
> I join the struggle
> Of love's triumph over greed
> Spending myself for the captive
> Praying that more liberators will be sent
> Until every slave is free.

After a few words of encouragement, Dani dismissed us into smaller groups for a twenty-minute check-in. Each facilitator used a list of simple questions to help guide discussion:

- How successful were you this week with enacting the changes in spending and consuming that you committed to?

- How did your period of prayer and fasting go? What kind of fast did you choose?

- Talk about the most significant thing you learned this week in your research about human trafficking.

The room was buzzing with conversation when Sarah announced it was time to come back together. Representatives from an organization we would be volunteering with the following week had come to tell us about their work supporting local victims of human trafficking. They explained that there are myths surrounding sex and prostitution that perpetuate the exploitation of women. One myth is that women voluntarily choose to go into prostitution because they enjoy having anonymous sex or because the work is financially lucrative. The caseworker told us that most, if not all, of the women who enter their program became involved in prostitution through force, manipulation, financial desperation or addiction. "These women," she said, "are victims of human trafficking, whether they have been transported across international borders or were domestically coerced into prostitution by a family member or boyfriend. A second myth," she said, "relates to the men who feed the demand for sexual services. They come from the entire spectrum of socioeconomic and cultural backgrounds. Many of them have a mistaken notion about masculinity, believing that having sex with multiple partners makes them more virile or manly."

I was so stirred by what I heard that I quickly typed a few lines into my online status: "An important aspect to addressing sex trafficking is confronting our cultural myths about manhood and sexuality. Women want to be loved and cherished, not objectified. Real manhood is not about multiple sexual conquests, but honor and fidelity. This means, for instance, that pornography is not only an issue of personal morality but also of justice and human rights."

After their presentation and some Q and A, Sarah explained the story of Jesus and the woman at the well from John 4 as an example of victimization: "In a male-oriented society where women were easily divorced and made vulnerable, this woman was living intimately with a man she wasn't married to—most likely out of desperation, after being divorced by five previous husbands. Only a shunned and disgraced woman would come to fetch water at the warmest time of day. Jesus loved this 'unclean' Samaritan woman in a countercultural way by speaking with her, affirming her dignity and worth."

Sarah divided us into pairs and invited us to go out into the streets in search of the Samaritan woman—meaning someone involved in the sex industry: "Try to meet someone and recognize their dignity and worth as Jesus did in this story."

Adam, my partner for this exercise, and I left the building and quickly walked toward an intersection where we found ourselves standing in front of a massage parlor. I hesitantly pushed the doorbell on a locked metal gate. Shortly the latch buzzed and we made our descent down a set of stairs, around a blind corner and into a makeshift waiting room hidden from street view. We were greeted by a woman in her early sixties, wearing heavy makeup, high heels and lingerie. "You want massage?" she asked, mentioning a price, and added, "We have many pretty girls for you!" We politely excused ourselves and rushed up the stairs. My heart was breaking. Who knew it would be so easy to enter the domain of sexual slavery? Here we were, standing only feet away from trafficked girls who were kept hidden behind locked gates.

A few minutes later, two women from our project rang the doorbell at the same location but were brusquely told, "We are busy and can't help you," confirming our suspicion that the true nature of the business was sexual rather than therapeutic.

We continued walking down the street, past strip clubs where burly men invited us to see eighteen-year-old girls dancing naked on the stage. I looked into the eyes of two young women standing shyly behind one of the doormen. Despite their high heels and mini dresses, they carried themselves like self-conscious high school girls, wearing heavy makeup to cover lingering teenage acne.

At nine o'clock we gathered back at Cameron House to compare notes from our expeditions. Sarah asked us to take a few minutes by ourselves to write a poetic prayer about what we had just experienced. In my journal I wrote,

> God, my heart is breaking. My heart is breaking because I live in a city where fifty dollars can fetch you thirty minutes of pleasure by the scared hands of an undocumented woman. My heart is breaking because I live in a town where, for less than the price of a movie ticket, you can watch an eighteen-year-old girl strip away her dignity. My heart is breaking be-

cause I live in an age when you can vicariously participate in any of these activities for free, in the privacy of your own home, from any computer or phone with Internet connectivity. My heart is breaking because I know that I am pulled between honoring, objectifying and despising the Samaritan woman. My heart is breaking because I realize that the root of human slavery is the human heart, wanting to possess what it has not earned by love, trust and fidelity.

As we shared our poetic prayers and recounted the tales of our encounters, the emotional pitch in the room became palpable. A few of us began to cry. Some of us were moved because we were facing our own impulses to regard people as objects; others were moved because we knew what it was like to be that vulnerable boy or girl whose dignity has been violated by an act of greed.

The building where we met is named for Donaldina Cameron, a courageous young missionary who began rescuing girls trafficked to San Francisco for prostitution in the 1870s. At the close of our meeting we descended three flights of stairs to an underground tunnel where Donaldina had kept the girls when their "owners" came looking for them. We took turns crawling up into the narrow passageway to see where liberators who came before us had welcomed, protected and cared for the Samaritan woman.

## Dynamics of Transformation

*I am making everything new!*

Revelation 21:5

In the example of the open-invitation group experiment above, you may notice various elements that were included in the evening: prayer, small group check-in and discussion, Scripture and teaching, new information, an action-based response, and creative reflection. Though this was an especially poignant session, we try to be holistic in our approach to any experiment, engaging as many aspects of transformation as possible. Here are the dynamics we try to keep in mind whenever we are designing an experiment.

1. *Transformation happens through new vision.* Change really begins with new vision, beliefs and perspectives. Through group experiments we give one another an opportunity to respond, in some specific way, to the countercultural reality of God's kingdom. The vision that inspired our Abolition project was that God is active in our world and invites us to be agents of healing and justice. We find it helpful and necessary to regularly remind each other of the larger vision that motivates our shared actions and practices. Crafting a prayer that embodies our vision and repeating it at the beginning and end of each session helps us stay conscious of the connection between what we do and why we do it.

2. *Transformation happens through new experiences.* Action brings true understanding of what it means to practice the way of Jesus. When we risk going new places, meeting new people and risking new activities the resulting disequilibrium can create space for change. New experiences challenge our assumptions and beliefs, help us face our fears and surprise us with resources and strength we didn't know we had.

Imagine how different our Abolition project would have been if we had stayed inside the building or met in a more safe or convenient neighborhood. Hearing firsthand accounts, seeing places where trafficking occurs and meeting affected people made the need and opportunity for action much more urgent and tangible. The Scriptures become more alive and relevant to us when we can connect them with real people and places. Live encounters take us out of the realm of theory and rhetoric and give us a living story to tell. We are after the kind of firsthand experience with God's reality that John the disciple described: "[That] which we have heard, which we seen with our own eyes, which we have looked at and our hands have touched—this we proclaim concerning the Word of life" (1 John 1:1). After our project was completed, several participants went on to become more deeply involved in trafficking advocacy and prevention.

3. *Transformation happens through establishing new patterns of thought and action.* We are, by nature, creatures of instinct and habit, who have inherited and developed patterns of thinking and acting that determine who we are and who we are becoming. For the Abolition experiment, we invited each other into several new ways of thinking and doing. We asked each other to fast one day a week and to change our patterns of consumption. We worked at seeing people involved in the sex industry through eyes of compassion. Disciplines of engagement (like service) or abstinence (fasting) make us more aware of our automatic responses and help us develop new and healthier choices.

4. *Transformation happens through group encounter and reflection.* We are much more likely to take steps to change in solidarity with others. Consider how often Jesus invited his disciples into practices with him (like prayer or Sabbath keeping) or sent them out to preach and heal in teams. Most of us simply don't have the courage, discipline or self-awareness to change or grow on our own. Abolition, in particular, was an experiment that could really only be done safely and wisely in a group.

The time we spend in small group reflection is an important aspect of the process that provides accountability and support for the new choices and risks we are taking. We integrate what we learn more fully by reflecting on the shifts happening internally.

For many of us the project brought up many issues or questions. For instance, in small groups some of us confessed that we didn't keep the fast or make the consumer changes we committed to. For others the sorrow we felt for victims during the project became overwhelming, and we had to learn to seek God's peace and comfort in a new way.

Some of us naturally reflect on our experiences, while others need help to meaningfully process what we are getting in touch with. A good question can help: "What do you think makes it difficult for you to follow through on your commitments?" Or, "How do you think God can help you face your fears?" Where possible, we try to include creative activities, like a poetry exercise, to help each other integrate and reflect on what we are learning.

"Every year I feel myself becoming a worse person," lamented Jackie, a twenty-five-year-old wrestling with the growing complexities of adult life. "It was so much easier to feel like I was doing good and pleasing God when I was younger." Jackie wasn't necessarily a better person before, she was simply less aware of herself. We are prompted to seek deeper heart change as we get more in touch with our true condition. Self-awareness is only a step toward becoming God-aware. Deeper questions are "What is my Creator inviting me into?" and "What is my next immediate step toward practicing the way of Jesus?"

When we see the difference between where we are and who we were made to be, it's easy to become discouraged or give up. We can learn to see self-awareness as a gift, and the conviction to live differently as a gentle invitation from One who knows us completely.

*5. Transformation happens through good examples and guidance.* Having a team of five or six people with high levels of investment and expertise to guide our project was important. Imagine twenty, thirty or fifty people trying to take action together without a clear sense of leadership or vision. Having a small, collaborative team think through the steps freed the group to focus on the action at hand, rather than filling time trying to decide what to do. It is crucial with a project like this to have people leading who have a certain amount of experience and credibility with the topic, and the skills and confidence to help others process their experiences.

*6. Transformation happens through failures, setbacks, mistakes and persistence.* After my brief and awkward encounter with the older woman at the massage parlor I was left to wonder, *Did I really treat her as God's beloved daughter? Was I so quick to leave because I was shocked, appalled or scared?* At the end of the Abolition project, having learned about the scope of human trafficking, several participants expressed deep disappointment. "Did we really accomplish anything?" they wondered. "We barely scratched the surface of what needs to be done." These were good questions to wrestle with and help one another navigate.

We learn and grow as much from our failures as from our successes. Failure and mistakes are part of training to do something new. Though it's not really failure if you are learning by trial and error—unless you quit trying. When we are experimenting with new ways of being and doing, we shouldn't be surprised when we don't do well. Anything worth doing can be done badly at first. We are all beginners at learning to follow the loving ways of the Rabbi.

In the Gospels we often see the early disciples of Jesus trying and "failing." One time Jesus came upon a scene where they were arguing with a crowd. A demon-possessed boy had been brought to them and they weren't able to heal him. Exasperated, Jesus commanded the demon to leave. Later they asked, "Why couldn't we drive it out?" Jesus said, "This kind can only come out by prayer" (Mark 9:14-29). The disciples didn't know what they didn't know and this disappointing experience helped them learn how to rely on God's power more effectively in the future.

One of the surprising lessons from our Abolition project was the challenge we had working together as a team on something we were all so passionate about. We had differences of opinion about how the project should be managed, who was responsible for specific details, who should lead up front and whether our contributions or expertise were adequately valued. When we are on a journey together there are going to be misunderstandings. While working closely on a project our personal wounds, insecurities or brokenness become more easily exposed. This phenomenon is predictable enough that we've named it "The dojo you didn't choose, that chooses you." The growth that comes from working through team conflict can be as transformational as the project itself.

7. *Transformation into the likeness of Christ happens by the power of the Spirit.* One participant in our Abolition project thought that instead of focusing on intentional practices and public actions we should spend more of our time praying for victims of trafficking and their oppressors. "What about the Spirit?" she asked rather indignantly, suggesting that our efforts were in competition with God's activity. We are challenged not to create a false dichotomy between our actions and the work of the Spirit—that "it's all up to God," or "it's all up to us." Jesus told his disciples to practice the teachings and rely on the leading and power of the Spirit. The Spirit is at work any time transformation into Christlikeness takes place. We are invited to do whatever we can to surrender to the work of the Spirit in us, and pray and expect God's kindness to also lead others toward transformation.

8. *Transformation is rooted in the heart.* When some people involved with Abolition found out how victims were being treated in the massage parlors, they were ready to knock down the doors and rescue the girls by force. We had to talk them down by explaining that this wouldn't solve the problem and might further endanger the women. One of the more profound, if painful, insights from the project was that human trafficking is one obvious example of the pervasiveness of human lust and greed. Significant healing change will only come as each person involved in the supply and demand cycle makes different choices. This includes each of us. You and I may not participate directly in human trafficking, but as consumers we all desire goods and services at prices that will not provide for acceptable and safe working conditions. And by passive indifference we participate in aspects of our culture

that objectify people as commodities of desire. Changing public policy and opinion can help, but the root cause lies within the human heart.

The heart is the control center of the whole person, the place from which we decide what to think, how to feel and what to do. Jesus said, "Where your treasure is, there your heart will be also" (Luke 12:34) and "out of the overflow of the heart the mouth speaks" (Matthew 12:34). Our actions express the intentions of our hearts. A group practice doesn't guarantee a change of heart for anyone, but it does create a supportive environment where transformation is likely to occur. Experiments can expose where heart renovation is needed. Real substantive change occurs as we learn to surrender to the will and authority of the Creator from the core of who we are. A change of heart can begin inwardly or outwardly, but always involves surrendering to the will and power of God.

## Discussion

- *Integration.* How would you explain the connection between inward practices (like prayer) and outward practices (like service)?

- *Finding balance.* Which comes easier to you, outward activism or inward discipline? Do you feel a tension between the two? In what way? How would you like to navigate the tension between these dimensions better or differently?

- *Abolition project.* What struck you as the most interesting or curious aspect of the Abolition project described in this chapter? What questions or concerns came to mind? Describe a similar experiment you've been a part of, or imagine what participating in such an experiment would be like for you.

- *Meeting elements.* What sticks out to you in how the group interacted as they went through the Abolition experiment? How are these similar or different from the activities in the groups you have been part of? How do you think they enhanced the experience for group members?

- *New experiences.* Describe a time when a new experience or risk created space for transformation in your life.

- *Failure.* Think of a time when you took a risk of obedience and the results were disappointing. How might we create environments where we feel free to try new things and even make mistakes?

- *Rooted in the heart.* What do you think is necessary to having a change of heart? How would you describe the posture of your heart right now?

## Exercise

*Read the account from John 4* in which Jesus crossed boundaries of race, gender and social class to connect with the Samaritan woman. Discuss the story and come up with a one-time practice with a small group of friends. Who would the people around you be most surprised to see you chatting with? What kind of person is typically mocked or despised by your tribe? Commit to engaging someone this week who is distant from you culturally or socio-economically.

# 6

# Initiating and Leading Group Experiments

*My mother and brothers are those who hear God's word and put it into practice.*

Luke 8:21

When I was five years old, my dad decided it was time for me to learn how to ride a bicycle. I grew up in a city with extensive paved trails around its rivers and lakes, and my dad had a dream for us to be a bicycle-riding family. I vividly remember going with him to the shop where he bought me a metallic gold Schwinn bicycle with upright handlebars and a sparkling gold banana seat. I had seen my dad pedaling effortlessly on his bicycle and as we drove home I pictured myself gliding along the sidewalk. When we unloaded my new bicycle I was anxious to take it for a spin. My dad helped me get on and ran beside me holding onto the seat while I pedaled. It felt just like I had imagined, until he let go and I immediately crashed into the cement, badly skinning my knees and elbows. He picked me up and made me try a few more times before I gave up, sobbing. Riding a bicycle wasn't as easy as it looked. We went back to the store and bought training wheels, which I used for several months. I still fell down a hundred times before I finally learned how to keep my balance. But the spills I took as I learned how to ride pale in comparison to all the fond memories I have of cycling with my dad.

Learning to initiate and lead shared practices can be a bit like learning to ride a bicycle—it takes practice and may require training wheels and a few spills along the way. Sometimes the difference between failure and success is in understanding balance and the details of technique. In this chapter we will explore some of those details along with a few things we wish we had known when we began.

## Where to Begin

A first step is for those who aspire to lead to personally make a commitment to a shared experimental approach for their own spiritual development. You can't lead someone else to a place you've never been yourself. Leaders can invite small groups of people into a series of short-term experiments or practices that can eventually be shared with a wider audience. It is best to begin with a person-centered or group-initiated experiment (see chapter two) to gradually build the confidence and finesse to initiate an open-invitation experiment.

A second step is to publicly cast a vision for what life in the kingdom can look like, and how shared practices help us experience that reality. If you have done a few more private experiments, you will have firsthand stories of transformation to tell that will inspire people to get involved. Then you can begin offering a cycle of experiments and let momentum spread through your network and community.

Another approach is to inspire and train a group of leaders and educators to integrate a practice-based approach within existing groups by seeding the question "What is one thing we can each commit to do before our next meeting to apply the reality of the gospel to the details of our lives?" A resource like this book might be good for a group of leaders to read and work through together.

Again, most people will have to experience action- and practice-based learning before they are able to help someone else practice and teach the Way.

## Identifying Collaborators

It can be scary to initiate something new, but even more so to do it alone. I can't stress enough how important it is to have partners—one or two people you trust who share a common vision and readiness for action. When you collaborate you have a greater pool of skills and wisdom to draw from, and a wider network of potential participants to invite. Ideally, women and men will both be represented. You might also include one or two "apprentices" who are just beginning to develop their leadership potential. By collaborating, the very act of initiating can be a shared experiment in itself, even if no one else ends up joining you.

With any open-invitation experiment that I've been a part of there are usually two lead partners and two or three other collaborators. As you form your team, there are several important questions to consider. First, do we have the time and stability in our lives to lead this practice well? With their first open-invitation group experiment many people discover that leading a practice takes more time and energy than they initially expected. Second, do we have the skills that are needed—including the ability to gather people, plan, organize and facilitate? It is better to start out small and build your confidence and credibility than to begin by trying to guide a larger group. To initiate a practice, you don't have to be an expert, but it's helpful if the team has some prior experience. If the practice you want to invite people into is new to you, let participants know this from the start and don't present yourself as an expert. Third, do we have a healthy understanding of leadership that balances the need for clear direction with providing a warm and safe environment? Those of us who are used to leading from the top sometimes find it difficult to make the adjustment to a collaborative and participatory team. Others of us, in reaction to negative leadership experiences, might feel hesitant to provide clear direction when it is appropriate and necessary. Be aware of your leadership strengths and weaknesses. Finally, it's helpful to ask, "Are we each growing in integrity in our apprenticeship to Jesus and our reputations with others?" To have authenticity and credibility, your leadership has to come from lived experience that gives you the confidence to say, "Follow my example, as I follow the example of Christ" (1 Corinthians 11:1).

## Designing Your Experiment

Once you've identified your collaborators, the next step is to design your experiment. Pray and brainstorm some ideas together. After exploring the options, identify the one idea that has the most energy and consensus among you to move forward with. If you are new to initiating experiments it may be best to start with a practice you are already familiar with. Creating your first experiment from scratch will add an extra layer of work and planning that might be better saved for after your group dynamics and culture have been established. A good place to begin might be to review the experiments described in part two of this book and pick one that seems most appealing to your team. But note that any experiment ideas you borrow from this material or other places will need to be personalized to fit your group and context.

You will want to name the aspect of the vision and teachings of Jesus you hope to investigate and explore how this theme intersects with your felt needs and common concerns. Recall the five basic themes of human experience that the teachings of Jesus address, which are summarized by the Lord's Prayer: identity, purpose, security, community, and freedom and peace. Perhaps you've noticed or been a part of groups oriented around one or two of these dimensions. We tend to emphasize aspects of the teachings of Jesus that naturally appeal to us and neglect those that don't.

To pursue a balanced approach to spiritual formation we've created an annual cycle of experiments that reflect each of these five themes. Each year we examine the specific instructions Jesus gave within these dimensions and develop a shared practice. At the beginning of an experiment it's really helpful to spend some time reflecting on the specific commands of Jesus. A summary list of these instructions for each theme of the Lord's Prayer is included in the next five chapters. Whenever I look at the list of things Jesus instructed his disciples to do, I'm struck with bewilderment and awe—we are truly being invited into a whole new way to be human.

Once you have identified a theme and a shared practice, you can think through the specific details of your experiment. What are the three or four main goals of the project? Is it a one-time action or multiweek experiment? Who will you invite to join you? Where is the most appropriate place to meet? What exercises do you plan to do during the sessions and what will participants be required to do on their own during the week? One of the early mistakes we made was creating experiments that were too complicated. We gradually learned that limiting ourselves to one or two compelling practices was better than having people feel overwhelmed. Finally, it's critical to decide what tasks and roles each collaborator needs to fulfill to execute the plan. To avoid stress and confusion, it can be helpful to develop a timeline for when certain tasks need to be completed. When you are asking participants to trust you with their time and resources, it's important to be well prepared and organized. A certain degree of formality that might not be familiar can be helpful to establishing a culture of intentional experimentation and practice.

## Inviting People into Your Experiment

After you've brainstormed the details of your experiment, write up a short description of the vision, goals and details to share with the people you plan to invite (see the appendixes of this book for several examples). The most effective way to involve people in your experiment is to invite them personally through a note or phone call. You might also announce the project to a larger constituency through public messages and social-networking tools. We usually link our experiments to an online registration page that makes it clear how to sign up and pay any fees. You want the invitation to be clear and concise so that potential participants easily understand the vision and expectations of the experiment before they arrive.

We learned the hard way that it's not effective to force an experiment onto an unsuspecting person or group. It's important to give people a chance to opt in. You may be surprised by who does or does not choose to participate. Not everyone is ready for intentional, shared practices. When given the choice between a context that requires high commitment and one that promises belonging without participation, most people will choose the one that requires the least amount of effort. There is an inherent tension between our impulses to belong and our desire to become. When we invite one another into shared practices we are asking people to say yes or no to a defined path. Thousands of people flocked to hear Jesus, hundreds stayed to ask questions and just a few dozen chose to become his disciples. Perhaps this is why Jesus said that his teaching would create divisions among families (Matthew 10:34-35). Practicing the way of Jesus will always be a minority activity—which suggests that we keep on "evangelizing" one another to risk being transformed by the power of the gospel.

Sharing a vision of life in the kingdom and inviting people into contexts where they can practice the teachings of Jesus is a way of announcing the good news. In the Great Commission Jesus gave his disciples, evangelism was not a discrete activity that could be separated from apprenticeship. He told his disciples to "go and make disciples . . . baptizing them . . . and teaching them to obey everything I have commanded you" (Matthew 28:19-20). The crisis of evangelism we face in the Western world is not a lack of information about the gospel, but a scarcity of examples of transformed people who would provoke others to ask, "How did you discover this remarkable new way of life?"

You can invite anyone to "try on" the teachings of Jesus. A person doesn't have to believe in Jesus before they can engage in group experiments or shared practices. Even the first disciples of Jesus became aware of the significance of who he was gradually. Their confidence in him grew as they saw how his teachings played out in real life.

Over the years our experiments have attracted three kinds of people: (1) church participants who want to go further in their discipleship, (2) "postcongregational" people who have a desire to follow Jesus but are skeptical about mainstream Christianity and (3) post-Christian seekers who have developed a curiosity about the way of Jesus. It is tricky navigating how to cultivate an environment where all three kinds of people feel safe. Our language and approach might be too Christocentric for some, not "traditional" enough for others, or more honest and gritty than is comfortable for another. A mixed environment, where we are all out of our comfort zones, can be a potent and dynamic space for transformation.

On the first night of Awakening Creativity, Ethan, a middle-aged gay man, introduced himself as a former Tibetan Buddhist monk newly curious about Jesus. He said he signed up for the project because it seemed different from a church service and a safe place to explore. When I referred to a Scripture passage as coming from "the Tanakh," several participants looked confused, but Ethan exclaimed, "It means a lot to me that you would say Tanakh instead of Old Testament. Thanks for respecting my Jewish heritage!" Three months later Ethan signed up for another learning lab and arrived the first evening wearing a Celtic cross, which he proudly showed me, explaining that he had become a Christian.

## Facilitating Sessions

When I'm leading a practice, my collaborators and I try to arrive well in advance of other participants to set up our space, check in as a team and pray together. We usually have a printed schedule and a two-page handout that includes some Scripture, discussion questions, homework assignments and other relevant material. Because we value a collaborative approach and want to see more people equipped to lead, we do our best to give everyone on the team a visible role during each session. There are a few basic tasks involved in guiding any experiment, including giving an orientation and sharing vision, leading specific exercises or practices, small group facilitation, hospitality, set-up and clean-up, and administration. If there are more than six or seven people involved in the experiment, we divide into smaller groups for check-in and some of our exercises so that everyone has adequate "air-time" to process and dialogue about their experience.

On the first night we try to create a welcoming environment by serving tea and a small, healthy snack. In a reminder email that goes out two days before, we let participants know that we plan to start promptly. After a welcome and prayer we ask everyone to introduce themselves and share what interested them in the project. Then we spend fifteen to twenty minutes explaining the vision of the project, the goals and expectations for participation, and give people a chance to ask questions and clarify anything they may not have understood. Then, if it is a multiweek experiment, we ask people to sign a contract of participation (see examples in the appendixes), emphasizing that it's okay for anyone to opt out after the first meeting if they don't feel like they are able to make a full commitment to the experiment. If they do decide to participate, we stress that it's important to be at each session. In our experience, we've come to expect that 5 to 10 percent of participants will drop out after the first or second week.

When we first began initiating experiments we were so eager to have as many people as possible participate that we let people casually drop in partway through the process. Of course, these people often didn't understand our vision and expectations and hadn't completed the practices the rest of us had, which made our check-ins awkward. Our guests ended up undermining the dynamics of the group and eventually we learned that to maintain momentum and intensity it was important to have clear entry and exit points.

In each session of a multiweek experiment we include prayer, restatement of vision, a small group check-in and an onsite practice or exercise. We've found that initiating a group experiment is a nuanced skill that is more complex than telling people what you know or dictating what they should do. The primary goal is not sharing information but inviting one another into action. When our projects haven't been well thought out, there has been a tendency to spend too much time discussing ideas without engaging in new practices together. We try to share only as much information as the group needs in order to have a vision to take action or begin a practice. Since most of us have full lives, we've learned to maximize the practice aspect of our time together, even if it means sitting quietly in a circle responding to reflection questions or writing poetry.

At the end of each session, we gather together to give direction on any homework and do some cheerleading. We like to give each collaborator a chance to offer a "coaching comment" to encourage the group or address an issue that has come up during the session. The day after the session we send a follow-up message to participants that includes a digital copy of the handout, a brief summary of the session and any additional coaching comments that will help them keep momentum on their individual practices. Most of us are well intentioned about fulfilling our commitments, but it's easy to forget, so we've learned to overcommunicate expectations and agreements to make it as easy as possible for people to remember what they have committed to do.

## Evaluation

At the beginning of the last session, or in the last hour of an intensive, we take ten to fifteen minutes to have each person fill out a written evaluation. Since we often have a potluck meal after the evaluation, people are highly motivated to complete it. By doing the evaluation when we are together we get more feedback and it helps prepare people for the verbal group processing that follows. The evaluation includes questions to help participants reflect on the results of their practice, and space to give organizers feedback about what activities were most effective and how the experiment might be made better in the future (see examples in the appendixes). The positive results people experience become the stories that seed wider participation in future experiments. Participants who have experienced deep transformation often become our collaborators for similar experiments the following year.

## Learning from Our Mistakes

With a how-to book like this it would be tempting to present an overly glossy picture of a technique that promises immediate success. But if you are like me, you are wary of easy answers and silver bullet solutions—knowing that real life is always more messy. Early readers of this book said, "We don't want to just hear stories about your successes—we can learn as much or more from your mistakes." The examples shared throughout this book were preceded by years of false starts, half-baked concepts and failed attempts to create community around shared practices. Looking back, I've learned to see these as precious events that helped us gain the momentum and balance needed for later achievements. You are going to make mistakes as you learn to initiate experiments. I hope that by sharing both our triumphs and spills, you can enjoy the transformational potency of shared practices—avoiding the mistakes we've made and making new ones that can add to a collective wisdom.

*Getting "unstuck."* One of my first challenges in creating space for shared practices was overcoming the tensions within myself. We don't generally look for new ways until we discover that a previous path has led to a dead end. The birth of something new often begins with grieving what you have left behind. I began trying to lead experiments partly out of my frustrations with the limited view of the gospel I had received earlier in life, and with the unfulfilling practices I'd been taught. When I realized that there was a better story and the possibility of a more integrative path, I felt both hopeful and angry. For many of us, deconstruction is a necessary part of the journey—though there is a danger of getting stuck in a state of reaction and negativity.

It was hard for me to get positive momentum on new and creative practices when I was living in regret about the time I'd spent on paths that now seemed fruitless. I was helped by having a group of friends and colleagues who were also yearning for new ways of seeking and leading. A group of us met once a week over three months to systematically work through the shifts we were experiencing. We gave each other permission to ask questions, wrestle with Scripture and experiment with new practices. Going through this process together grounded us, helped us know that we were not alone and gave us the supportive environment we needed to grieve and imagine new possibilities.

I remember when my friend Matt became stuck in the process of rethinking. After many years of leadership in larger churches, Matt and his wife, Kim, had become quite skeptical. Although they spent many hours helping with activities and programs, they felt deeply lonely, and wondered if anyone in their faith community really cared or desired to know them more intimately. This feeling only intensified when Kim had a mid-term miscarriage of their third child. "Is any of this really helping us grow spiritually?" they asked. "We feel hurried and caught up in the squeeze of raising kids and paying the mortgage. Is another sermon series or Bible study really going to fix the ache we feel inside?" When Matt and I went on long walks he would vent his frustrations and growing disillusionment. Once he asked, "If Jesus came to bring transformation to the whole person, why aren't we experiencing that more?" I encouraged Matt to consider how he might shift his attention from critiquing the current systems he was a part of to getting creative about how to cultivate a new path and practice. During that time their family joined one of our early tribe experiments. Gradually they recognized that what they were really searching for was a spiritual practice that was more rooted in the daily life of their family and neighborhood. They began inviting friends and neighbors to share meals in their home and learned to make community, prayer and service part of the natural rhythms of their family. Their anxiety and frustrations about "the church" began to fade as they realized they could take responsibility for their own growth and cultivate shared practices with friends, neighbors and other lonely people.

If you have had doubts or questions about the path you've been on, you are not alone. Most of us, at some point, will struggle with disappointments or stumble over the shortsighted ways we have understood God and God's kingdom. When this happens we can dismiss our earlier faith as naive, deny the ambiguities, or press into the questions to negotiate thriving belief. You can even make a shared practice of your disappointments and struggles by doing something proactive to get "unstuck." Gather with a group of friends who are feeling similarly deconstructed and meet six to eight times to work through your questions and doubts. Put a time limit on voicing your complaints. It may be appropriate to have a trusted guide facilitate a process of healing and restoration. You may also find that actively practicing the way of Jesus will turn the volume down on your negativity and frustrations.

***Structure and intentionality.*** Perhaps the most challenging obstacle I've had to overcome to be part of creating space for shared practices has been my own fear of structure. It has taken me a long time to recognize how much intentionality is needed in order to pursue life together in the kingdom of love. I naturally gravitate toward creative and open-ended situations and I tend to value relationships more than programs. For most of my twenties and early thirties I operated under the assumption that if we just "hang out and love Jesus," we would become like him with little direct guidance or organized effort. Part of this came from an idealism that I hope to never lose, but much of it was rooted in what I now see as life-stage naiveté and a lack of understanding about how life actually works. I'm sad to say that I hurt a lot of people because I didn't understand how clear structures that value relationships create a healthy environment for growth and change.

Many of the leaders I work with have a lot of passion and vision, but struggle to translate that into guiding a group toward intentional action. One of the greatest temptations of a leader is to talk about new ideas or share vision without providing a clear path for integrating learning into life. While dialogue may be an important step, it is stillborn unless it eventually leads to action. A renewed understanding of leadership is critical to creating space for whole-person discipleship. Leaders need to begin seeing themselves not just as hosts, caregivers or communicators, but also as initiators and coaches who invite people into compelling acts of obedience. Taking steps to obey Jesus and inviting others into a common journey is the best way to make disciples. I believe that even paid pastors can renegotiate their job descriptions to include devoting a significant portion of their work time to living out kingdom values in collaboration with others.

*Always a beginner.* A third issue I had to face was that even though I saw myself as a leader, I wasn't equipped to lead people in a way of practice. It was deeply revealing to recognize that my knowledge of the Bible, my experience as a pastor and my seminary education did so little to prepare me to lead people to do the things that Jesus did and taught. In the ways of the kingdom, my credibility wouldn't come from what I knew or how well I performed publicly, but from my lived experience, practicing and teaching the Way (Matthew 5:19). One of the common mistakes people make when initiating experiments is to try to lead out of their knowledge or ideals rather than their lived experiences. One day I had the epiphany that it will actually take me the rest of my life to become the kind of disciple I wish to be. Good leaders are committed learners.

An early mistake I made, and have seen others make, was to try to lead others into shared practices as if I didn't need to learn myself—to step outside the process as a facilitator. Making disciples is not like being a sports coach who can give drill instructions from the sidelines. People can sense whether you are "in" or "out." For me, experiments can never be something I do for other people without actively participating myself, because I still have so much more to learn about life in the kingdom of love. Of course, as an initiator I help guide the process, but I also set the standard for risk and obedience by my example, so I must be as committed, engaged and transparent as anyone else in the room. Perhaps Jesus warned his disciples not to call themselves "rabbi" or "teacher" because the posture of a beginner is the only way to be a disciple. I was, and still am, a beginner.

Now that we've explored a theological and practical orientation to shared practices, it's time to examine the teachings of Jesus more specifically. Each of the chapters that follow covers one dimension of life in the kingdom of love: identity, purpose, security, community, and freedom and peace. Examples of shared practices are included to seed your imagination for initiating and leading your own group experiments. It's now time to get on the bicycle and take a ride.

# Discussion

- *Riding a bicycle.* Recall learning to ride a bicycle. How long did it take you to master it? What was it like when you would lose your balance? What kept you committed to learning? In what way might mistakes be part of learning to practice the way of Jesus?

- *Identifying collaborators.* Think of three people you can imagine initiating an experiment with. What contribution would you bring to this team? What other competencies do you think would be needed?

- *Designing your experiment.* As you've read this book, what experiments have you been most attracted to? How would these experiments need to be modified to fit your context?

- *Inviting participants.* Who are the people or groups closest to you that might be interested in a shared practice? What do you think their questions might be? What would be the best way to introduce the idea?

- *Opting in.* Do you think someone has to identify as a Christian to participate in one of these experiments? What concerns you about people not wanting to join you in shared practices? How might inviting someone into a shared practice be like evangelism?

- *Facilitating sessions.* Which of these roles do you feel comfortable with? Why?
    - Giving orientation and vision
    - Leading specific exercises or practices
    - Facilitating small group interaction
    - Hospitality
    - Setting up and cleaning up
    - Administration

- *Overcoming obstacles.* Can you relate to any of the obstacles identified in this chapter? What are the challenges you think of when it comes to initiating and leading others to practice the way of Jesus together?

## Exercise

*Workshop an experiment.* Get together with one or two people and brainstorm an experiment that you might invite others into. For now, just focus on the process of brainstorming. You can decide later if this is an experiment you actually want to try. Use the following questions as a guide for your discussion:

- Which aspect of life do we want our experiment to address (identity, purpose, security, community, freedom and peace)?

- Which specific teachings of Jesus do we want to explore through a shared practice?

- How does this teaching intersect with our felt needs and the concerns of our world? Where does the teaching of Jesus subvert our commonly held notions or habits?

- What action or practice can we adopt to live into the reality of the kingdom that Jesus spoke of?

- Is this a one-time activity, short-term or long-term experiment?

- Would this work best as a person-centered, group-initiated or open-invitation experiment?

- What would be the main goals of our experiment?

- Who would we invite to practice with us?

- If we were to initiate this experiment, what roles would we each likely play?

# Part Two
# Practices

# 7

# Experiments in Identity

*For those who are led by the Spirit of God are the children of God. The Spirit you received does not make you slaves, so that you live in fear again; rather, the Spirit you received brought about your adoption. . . . And by him we cry, "Abba, Father." The Spirit himself testifies with our spirit that we are God's children.*

Romans 8:14-16

*Before dawn*
*The streets of the city*
*Lie silent*
*And I think of you*
*Leaving the house*
*for the lonely places*
*Where you caressed*
*The constant presence*
*of our common ancestor*
*In the quiet of early morning*
*Only a thin space separates*
*Earth from eternity*
*And within my beating chest*
*I hear your Ghost-voice*
*Calling*
*Waking me*
*with the invitation*
*to be still*

*I surrender to the whisper*
*Breathe the moist cool air*
*Bathe in the mist*
*that blankets the ground*
*like a warm, wet kiss.*
*What I want*
*Is what you desire*
*I give myself over*
*To your voice*
*and to your touch*
*opening myself up*
*to the inheritance of Sabbath rest*
*that makes this day pregnant*
*by the fertile seed*
*of one dream.*

Mark Scandrette, July 29, 2007

When I first met my friend Dieter, he was a well-known faith leader and an inspiring example of pioneering creativity and success. A sudden stroke recently left him significantly disabled, with a speech impediment and physical paralysis. Known for his ability to inspire and teach, with an exceptional gift for making people aware of God through musical worship, this stroke has simply been devastating.

*How would I cope if my work and identity were suddenly taken from me?* I wondered as I drove toward Dieter's house. When he got into the car I tried to fill the uncomfortable silence with questions and chatter. Patiently Dieter turned to me and said, "Talk . . . slow! We . . . go . . . slow. . . . Talking . . . with . . . me . . . will . . . be . . . relaxing. . . . OK?"

At the brewpub, we sat across from one another, working to communicate. "I'm in the winter now," he said. "The spring, the summer, they were . . . new and . . . exciting. The fall was still colorful. But here it is dark and cold. Someday you will be where I am—not knowing whether spring or summer will come again." His eyes filled with tears, as did mine.

"Where do you find God now?" I asked, tentatively.

"It's hard to talk about. I know God loves me—more than I ever thought before. My family . . . my friends are so important now. To love and be loved is what really matters to me. And I love the small things—this food and drink. Sunshine. Sleep. Walking my dog."

Dieter delighted to show me some of his recent photographs— strikingly simple images that convey beauty beyond words. At great cost, Dieter has taught me how to embrace the identity of a beloved child through the seasons and sufferings of life.

In a world where we claw to find significance through who we know or what we achieve, we are invited to discover our truest identity as the blessed and beloved children of God.

## Gardens and Lonely Places: How Jesus Modeled Intimacy with the Father

The baptism of Jesus provides a compelling picture of the kind of intimate union with God we were created for. As he stepped out from the water he heard a voice saying, "This is my Son, whom I love; with him I am well pleased" (Matthew 3:16-17). The Spirit then led Jesus into the wilderness where his identity as the beloved was tested. He emerged after forty days a resolute son prepared to do "his father's business." Subsequently, Jesus often withdrew to gardens and other lonely places. In the most difficult hours leading up to his arrest, torture and crucifixion, he went into a garden one last time, kneeling to pray, "Abba, not my will but yours be done." A hidden life of solitude fueled his courageous public acts of love and sacrifice.

✦     ✦     ✦

Early one winter morning I climbed the hill that overlooks the city, swathed in a blanket of chilling fog. As I made my ascent I meditated on what was spoken over Jesus at his baptism. I personalized these words to try them on for size, and repeated them slowly: "Abba, I am your child. You love me. With me you are well pleased."

The first two phrases, though almost too good to be true, felt warm and comforting as they passed my lips. I choked on the third, "with me you are well pleased." The Father was pleased with Jesus before he had done anything of public importance. Is it possible that the Father delights in and is pleased with me in the same way? Am I also the beloved?

## Awakening Creativity

Though we live in a world of wonders, sustained by the Creator's presence and love, most of us go through times when we ask, "Where is God?" Living in an age of skepticism and disbelief, it

## A Vision for Discovering Our Identity as God's Beloved: Who Are We?

You and I are intimately loved by a Creator who is closer than our very breath. We are not alone and we have not been abandoned. We don't have to earn, beg or appease God. We are beloved and cared for simply because we are God's children. We may have called another "Mother" or "Father," but our true parent and our real home is the eternal "Abba." We were made for intimate union with the Father, sourcing our life from God's life. Nothing else on earth can satisfy us. In faith we surrender to Jesus as our teacher, trusting that the one who made us always has our best interests in mind. This is why we are invited to pray and live the words "Our Father in heaven, hallowed be your name." An apprentice of Jesus learns to find their primary identity in communion with the triune God.

## What Jesus Instructs Us to Be and Do

Below are the instructions Jesus gave about embracing our identity as God's beloved children. What makes Jesus unique, among prophets and enlightened ones, is the claim that he is "the exact representation" of God's being (Hebrews 1:3), whose life and sacrifice show us what love looks like and how we can become "one" with our Creator (John 17:22-23). The Gospel writers invite us to trust Jesus as a reliable messenger of the Creator's reality, power and love. Rooted in history, seen as the fulfillment of ancient prophecies, performing miracle signs and healings, speaking with authority greater than formal religious leaders, raising the dead and being raised from the dead himself, Jesus attributed his abilities to his intimacy with and submission to the Father—promising that those who would follow after him would do "even greater things" (John 14:12).

The conspicuous lack of clarity and power so often experienced by contemporary seekers of Jesus suggests that we have yet to learn to abide in the presence of the Father in the way that Jesus did. The hurry, distraction and competing expectations so common in our society make finding space for God challenging. How can we abide in the power that is "making all things new"?

• *Reimagine! Be awake to God's care and activity in your life:* "The time has come. The kingdom of God has come near. Repent and believe the good news!" (Mark 1:15).

- *Believe that Jesus is a reliable messenger of the Creator's love and saving power:* "The work of God is this: to believe in the one he has sent" (John 6:29).

- *Be reminded of the sacrifice and stay connected to the source:* "Remain in me, as I also remain in you. No branch can bear fruit by itself; it must remain in the vine. Neither can you bear fruit unless you remain in me" (John 15:4-6). "Whoever eats my flesh and drinks my blood remains in me, and I in them" (John 6:56). "Do this in remembrance of me" (Luke 22:19).

- *Make Jesus your teacher:* "Take my yoke upon you and learn from me" (Matthew 11:29).

- *Pray about everything, calling on God as "Abba":* "This, then, is how you should pray: Our Father in heaven, hallowed be your name" (Matthew 6:9).

- *Pray confidently and without superstition:* "When you pray, do not keep on babbling like pagans, for they think they will be heard because of their many words. Do not be like them, for your Father knows what you need before you ask him" (Matthew 6:7-8).

- *Pray discretely and privately:* "When you pray, go into your room, close the door and pray to your Father, who is unseen. Then your Father, who sees what is done in secret, will reward you" (Matthew 6:5-6).

takes courage and work to navigate the truth that we are not alone and have not been abandoned. Jesus dares us to imagine and believe that God is here with us, actively engaged in our lives and bringing shalom to our world.

Imagination, creativity and the appreciation of beauty can be powerful tools for connecting our identity as God's beloved with the details of our daily lives—especially in an age when so many of us live largely disconnected from the natural world or at a pace that doesn't allow us to easily "taste and see" that God is good. Here's an example of an experiment designed to help participants wrestle with finding God amidst the details and drama of life.

The room is filled with the aroma of burning candles, freshly cut flowers, cheeses and chocolate-covered strawberries, laid out in a spread of appetizing food and drinks. The bass thump of South Asian tabla beats can barely be heard over the chatter of hundreds of merry guests. At this event, aptly named Sacraments of the Natural, art installations are displayed throughout the room, each made with earthen materials. The centerpiece is a series of provocative portraits of the eighteen participating artists, who take turns guiding guests through the room while others mount the stage to read or perform poetry, music and stories they have written.

It's hard to believe that preparations for this show began only six weeks before, when a random group of suburban homemakers, tradespeople, teachers, social workers and Silicon Valley technology professionals gathered for the first session of a six-week experiment called Awakening Creativity.

Hopeful but apprehensive, Kathryn signed up for the project as her first foray into community after she stopped going to church two years previously. She'd been disappointed by "Christians" but even more significantly, felt abandoned by God in the midst of a difficult season of life. On the first evening of the project she was primed to be critical, but was surprised by how different this was from her previous experiences of "church." The facilitator didn't use the kind of religious language she expected, and explained things in ways that drew her in: "The goal of this experiment is to pursue the link between creativity and spirituality. We were made in the image of a Creator with a capacity for creative action. Imagination shapes who you are becoming. Although many of us live with a certain degree of dissonance between our theological beliefs and our lived experiences, through creative exercises we hope to help each other learn to cultivate the skill of connecting what we believe about God (and the nature of reality) with what we experience with our five senses—recognizing God's presence in the natural world and God's care amidst the messy details of our lives."

The group was invited into a series of daily practices, Scripture readings, creative exercises and weekly adventures out in nature— which was especially relevant for people who spend most of their waking hours in front of computer screens. As someone with an M.F.A. in fine art, Kathryn was impressed that after the orientation they were directed to actually make art on the spot in response to the topic that was introduced: "Create something with the clay you've been given and tell us how this reveals something about yourself," and "In the next ten minutes write a poem about what moves you toward wonder . . . ready, set, go!"

The point seemed to be getting people out of their heads and into embodied creative risks, which for Kathryn was a welcome alternative to the other-worldly religious experiences she'd had. At the end of the evening a homework exercise was explained: "You were born into a particular time and place and people, with a unique personality and story. To more fully embrace your identity as God's beloved, you can learn to tell the tale of your life as a God-bathed story. In ancient times people would set up stones to mark these encounters. Your homework is to find a stone to represent a turning point in your life, a time when you became aware of God's care and presence, and write a two-page account of that event." This was a challenging assignment for Kathryn because finding God in her own story was exactly what she struggled with most.

The next week they met again in smaller groups to check in on daily practices and read their "stone of remembrance" stories. Many of the stories read like dramatic movie scripts: accounts of near-death experiences, the survival of breast cancer, the pain and transition of divorce, a fond childhood memory of riding a horse. In an evening filled with laughter, tears and grateful wonder, people shared deeply about themselves—and more honestly than Kathryn expected or had seen before. When Kathryn read her own rather melancholy story, she was surprised by the understanding and affirmation she received.

In another session, the homework was to come prepared to do a photo shoot: "Bring a costume and props to visualize the person you are when you live in the shadows away from God's light—and another costume that expresses the person you hope to become as you risk moving further into God's kingdom." While the exercise was being explained, Kathryn spoke up, "I'll be honest, I have a hard time believing that God is really at work in the world. Once I thought I heard God and took a bold risk and it was a complete failure that left me worn out and devastated." Without being patronizing, the facilitator gently suggested that there might be other ways for Kathryn to interpret her experiences—because the story of her life wasn't over yet.

On the evening of the photo shoot everyone came dressed in his or her costume. Debbie, a woman in Kathryn's group, explained her pose and props: "For my shadow portrait I'm dressed as a stern police woman, because I feel that when I live in fear I tend to judge, control and police everyone around me. For my future portrait I am generous and unafraid, a cheerful hostess sharing my culinary talents . . . and, of course, chocolate." A man named Paul described the inspiration behind his portraits: "I really struggle with feeling like a prisoner of time, the demands of my work and societal expectations. So for my shadow portrait I came dressed as a Mickey Mouse watch. When I embrace God's light, I am relaxed and at peace—so I'm pictured here riding my motorcycle shirtless and free!"

For Kathryn's shadow portrait she pulled nylon stockings over her face, making her image flat and blurred and then covered her eyes with her hands. For her second portrait she appeared bright and smiling holding a colorful leaf of spring kale and a pink rose near her cheek. Kathryn's portraits spoke for themselves and she offered no further explanation.

Everyone put effort into assembling art pieces from their exercises to display in the show. On the final week they worked together to set up the room like a contemporary gallery space for a reception Friday evening. Though typically a shy person, Kathryn stood near the entrance greeting guests. No less than fifteen people came to the show by her invitation, including a professor from her graduate program, a Muslim friend and several colleagues from work. She eagerly led them through the exhibit, explaining the meaning and story behind each of her pieces and introducing them to the other artists. Something had shifted for Kathryn during the learning lab, and at the end of the evening she explained, "This project helped me reconnect with God. It was a safe place to explore. In my more 'churchy' days I always felt like my efforts to share my experience of God felt forced. Tonight I could be authentic with my friends about my spiritual journey in a nonthreatening way. We had some great conversations—and I don't think it even made my atheist friends feel weird."

The prayer the group prayed at the beginning and end of each session was displayed by the entrance to the exhibit, and aptly expressed the vision for Awakening Creativity:

> Created to be creative
> We enact our destiny
> Embracing the energy of the Spirit
> to risk making beauty with our whole lives.
> —*Mark Scandrette and Adam Klein*

## Entering Silence

*Very early in the morning, while it was still dark, Jesus got up, left the house and went off to a solitary place, where he prayed.*

Mark 1:35

What if instead of talking about prayer we actually prayed? That was the question we began with as we planned our first weekend silent retreat. Knowing that Jesus often withdrew to lonely places to pray, we wondered how we could learn this way together. Some of us had dabbled with a few hours of solitude, and one or two of us had done individual silent retreats, but for most of us this would be our first experience of extended silence and solitude. We didn't know exactly how it would go, inviting a whole group of people into this practice, but were willing to take a risk.

Through a friend we found a large place to stay at a beach house along the Pacific, just over an hour from the city where most of us lived. We started inviting friends, planned a simple, healthy menu and shopped for groceries. A few others assembled a collection of our favorite psalms and classical prayer exercises and drafted a schedule.

By Friday evening seventeen of us had gathered as a group that included single people, married couples, several older adults and a family with three school-aged children. We began with a meal, introductions and the question "What do you hope to be the outcome of your time of silence, solitude and prayer over the next thirty-six hours?" Zack wanted clarity about an upcoming decision about whether to continue in his job or go to graduate school. Nicole struggled with feeling close to God and hoped that an extended time would facilitate a breakthrough. Kevin, recently divorced, needed some space to heal and gain some perspective away from the bustle of the city. For others, the weekend was simply a chance to take another step in following the example of Jesus.

Sean handed out the retreat guide we had developed, which provided a basic schedule, a variety of prayer exercises, relevant Scripture portions and some journaling questions. The two of us gave a brief orientation to the historic practice of silence and solitude and its relevance for today, and answered questions about sleeping arrangements and mealtime duties. We asked each other to follow a few simple rules like, "turn off your cell phone" and, obviously, "no talking." We made the suggestion that people avoid reading books, because for many of us reading would be a convenient distraction from actually being present to God. After a group prayer, we began our vow of silence that would continue until Sunday at noon.

The house quickly became quiet as we settled into voicelessness. Some people dutifully pored over the retreat guide. Others began journaling in earnest or went out for a solitary walk in the moonlight. You could see that it took others time to gear down and they busied themselves in the kitchen or flipped through their Bibles. By Saturday afternoon most of us had relaxed and become comfortable, taking walks on the beach or napping in the sunlight. More than a few of us took multiple naps that day! It was surprising how easy it was to adjust to being silent in the company of others, especially sitting at the table together, slurping soup. Even the children found ways to observe the practice and occupy themselves—with only occasional whispers to parents and walks down to the village for ice cream. The initial novelty of silence had worn off by Saturday evening, and a somberness settled over the house.

When we broke the silence by celebrating the Lord's Table on Sunday, people were eager to share about their experiences. One person exclaimed, "I've been on many retreats, but this is the first time I will actually go home feeling more rested and refreshed! The lack of distractions really helped me relax." Nicole said that the most difficult time was Saturday night: "I started to feel lonely and had to face God and myself in ways that I usually avoid." And Zack added, "It was comforting to be in close proximity to other people pursuing the same goal. I don't know if I could have done this alone." As we finished our reflection, our last question to one another was, "How can we bring more space for silence, solitude and prayer into our everyday lives?"

## Embracing Stillness

*If you remain in me and my words remain in you, ask whatever you wish, and it will be done for you. This is to my Father's glory, that you bear much fruit, showing yourselves to be my disciples.*

John 15:7-8

Below is a description of an experiment in stillness prayer called Seeking the Kingdom Within that can be done as a one-time, forty-five-minute group exercise or a four- to six-week daily practice with weekly check-ins and group practice.

One by one people trickled into the room, and after everyone had had a chance to get a cup of tea the session began. Rick, my cofacilitator, welcomed the group and asked everyone to introduce themselves by sharing what they hoped to get out of our time together. Michael, who had been a spiritual seeker in the Tibetan Buddhist tradition for many years and had recently converted to the Orthodox church, said, "I'm here because I really enjoy being with the people in this room and I want to learn more about how to pray as a Christian." Jason shared that he had been feeling "pretty distant" and hoped for a breakthrough in his relationship with God. Camille went next, explaining that she had been wrestling with big questions about God and processing some emotional wounds from childhood: "I hope I can get some healing through prayer—and that being in this group will help me do that." Sophia, who went last, said, "I feel stuck. I'm not sure what I'm supposed to feel when I pray or whether I'm doing it right . . . and I know prayer isn't about how you feel. But, well, I guess I have a lot of questions."

"I'm glad that all of us are here," Rick said with a smile, pausing to look intently at each person in the circle. "One thing you might have noticed during our introductions is that we come from many different backgrounds and spiritual traditions—

which means that we may be at very different places on the journey. As you share, please don't assume that the person next to you has had the same experiences that you have, positive or negative, with the church or Christianity."

Then I began an orientation to the practice. "This is one in a series of learning labs we offer that explore various dimensions of the life and teachings of Jesus. We like to think of it as a 'Jesus dojo,' a space to practice what Jesus did and taught about life in God's kingdom. In the Gospels we see Jesus living in conscious awareness and surrender to the Father. With this experiment we'd like to take another next step into the reality he experienced and taught. So although we will be discussing various themes of prayer from the Scriptures and tradition, the main goal is to spend thirty to fifty minutes in each session practicing stillness prayer.

"Although there are many good ways to pray, for this experiment we are going to focus on one specific aspect of prayer—learning to be silent and still—with the goal of being aware of God's presence and the voice of the Spirit. Through this practice we hope to become more conscious of the Creator who is closer than our very breath. We call this experiment Seeking the Kingdom Within because once when Jesus was asked about the kingdom of God he responded, 'The kingdom of God does not come with your careful observation, nor will people say "here it is," or "there it is," because the kingdom of God is within you' [Luke 17:20-21 NIV 1984]. Similarly, the apostle Paul proclaimed, 'In God we live and move and have our being' [see Acts 17:28]. How can we learn to pay attention to the Spirit of God that is already living inside of us? An ancient psalm instructs us to 'be still, and know that I am God' [Psalm 46:10]. Perhaps you are already aware that stillness and silence were important practices in both historic Jewish and early Christian traditions.

"I want to give you another image of what stillness prayer represents. Think back to the account of Adam and Eve in the Garden after they had eaten fruit from the tree of the knowledge of good and evil. It was the cool of the day and the Creator was calling out, 'Adam, where are you?' They were hiding in the bushes, covering themselves with leaves. Who had withdrawn? Was it God? No, Adam and Eve were the ones who pulled away. Nothing, including their disobedience or shame, could keep the Creator from continuing to pursue relationship. Even now we are being invited to step out of the shadows and into the light of God's loving presence. For many generations we have been on the run from God, both in our minds and in our bodies. This posture of hiding is what keeps us from being more aware of God's care and presence. The prophet Isaiah once said, 'In repentance and rest is your salvation, in quietness and trust is your strength, but you would have none of it' [Isaiah 30:15].

"The first step in practicing stillness prayer is to become still in your body. The Hebrew word for 'repent,' *shuvah,* literally means 'to return.' Choosing to be still can be seen as a physical act of repentance—a bodily statement that you are no longer on the run, but returning to the love and care of your Creator. We do many things with our minds and bodies to distract ourselves from God's presence. The pace of life in our society and the pervasiveness of media and technology make it challenging to find space to hear God's voice. It is countercultural and it takes immense courage to be quiet in body and mind. For this exercise, you will want to get into a posture where you can sit comfortably and stay alert for thirty to forty minutes. For some people standing works better than sitting.

"A second step to practicing stillness prayer is to quiet your mind. To do this, focus on your breathing. The Creator formed you and brings life to you, by breath. It may be helpful to use a 'breath prayer': either a favorite name you use to cry out to God, like 'Father,' 'Jesus,' 'Abba' or 'Daddy,' or a short text of Scripture. Here are a few that I've found helpful. From the Psalms: 'I have stilled and quieted my soul; like a weaned child with its mother, like a weaned child is my soul within me' [Psalm 131:2 NIV 1984]. From the Gospels, the simple prayer of a tax collector: 'Lord have mercy on me' [*Kyrie eleison* in Greek; Luke 18:13]. Called the Jesus Prayer in Eastern Orthodox tradition, "Lord, Son of God, have mercy on me, a sinner" was popularized by the nineteenth-century Russian story called *The Way of a Pilgrim*. It even figures largely in the J. D. Salinger novel *Franny and Zooey*. 'In you I live and move and have my being' [Acts 17:28] is a personalized phrasing of the apostle Paul's speech in Athens. Another from the Psalms is a prayer of examen: 'Search me, God, and know my heart; test me and know my anxious thoughts' [Psalm 139:23]. One of my favorite breath prayers is very primitive; it's Hagar's exclamation when she encountered God in the desert: 'You are the God who sees me' [Genesis 16:13]. You might find it helpful to slowly meditate on one of these prayers, as you breathe in and out, to help you become more attentive to God."

Then Rick offered a bit of advice: "You might think of breath prayer like this. Sometimes when I'm driving in the car with my son, Jacob, he will say, 'Daddy, Daddy,' and I'll turn and say, 'Son, what is it?' Many times he calls my name just to know I'm there. It's acknowledgment, not vain repetition. Sometimes when I try to pray in stillness my mind immediately races with compulsive or negative thoughts, lists of things I have to do, anxieties, memories and disappointments, or a song from the radio that suddenly pops into my head. The act of stillness reveals the chaos and distractions of our minds and the patterns of thought that reflect our flight from God. Don't try to ignore or suppress those thoughts; acknowledge that they are there, but don't attach yourself to them. Surrender them to God and return to your breath and your awareness of God. In other words, 'take captive every thought to make it obedient to Christ'" (2 Corinthians 10:5).

I asked if anyone had any questions. Sophia shared about her previous experiences with stillness prayer, and Michael, who had read the early church fathers extensively, mentioned several nuances within the Hesychast tradition.* Rick gently guided the conversation to a close, "Well, there is so much we could discuss, but let's go ahead and give the practice a try." He lit a candle and turned down the lights as the group got comfortably situated, with some people sitting on chairs, others on pillows and Sophia standing. It got very quiet, and we suddenly became aware of the hum of a refrigerator, the occasional shifting or cough and the rumble of traffic outside. At one point Michael's stomach rumbled loudly, eliciting a few involuntary chuckles and breaking our concentration momentarily. After thirty minutes Rick said, "Okay, slowly open your eyes and come back into fuller awareness of the others in the room."

After everyone had a chance to stand and stretch, Rick asked, "How was that? Any thoughts or observations?" Jason said it seemed like a really long time—that just made him feel cold, sad and alone. Camille shared that she was able to calm her thoughts and feel God's presence in a way she rarely had before. And Sophia repeated her concern about wanting to pray the right way. Rick offered a few coaching comments, saying, "It's not always easy or fun to be present to God or aware of ourselves. Maybe that's why we so often keep ourselves distracted. Sometimes being still reveals the broken places where we need God's healing. If you find it difficult, try to let God meet you in your sadness, remembering that Christ also suffered and felt abandoned. He knows what you are feeling. There may also be times when you don't feel anything at all. Remember there is no such thing as the perfect way to pray. Learning to relax your expectations can help

---

*Hesychasm* is a Greek term for stillness, quiet or rest. It is used in Orthodox tradition dating from the fourth and fifth centuries, and is documented in *The Philokalia*. Closely related is the example and teachings of the Egyptian desert fathers (and mothers) from the third century who sought a prophetic life in the desert after Christianity was legalized by Constantine.

you to encounter God's grace and presence more fully. For some of us, it may take time to embrace that we really are cherished and beloved by our Creator."

Looking down at my watch I decided it was time to wrap up for the evening. "Okay, I think we are off to a good start. Let me reiterate the details of the experiment. We are each committing to practice stillness prayer for twenty minutes every day for the next six weeks. We will meet on the following five Tuesdays from seven o'clock until nine to sit for fifty minutes and discuss our experiences with the daily practice. Does that sound good to everyone?" There were nods all around. "I recommend that you pick a consistent time and place to pray each day. On Tuesdays, come prepared to check in about how your practice is going and what you are noticing. Remember, this kind of prayer is a lot like exercise—you'll notice the benefits through consistent repeated practice."

On the final week of our experiment we reflected together on our overall experience. Sophia had a subtle but significant breakthrough in her relationship with God. Camille found the practice helpful to her process of emotional healing. Through ongoing reflection and side conversations with Rick, Jason recognized that his difficulty with the practice may have been a symptom of deeper issues related to depression. Michael was enthusiastic about his experience. "As someone who has a rather stressful job as a home health nurse," he said, "I noticed that when I practiced consistently it helped me become more patient and present during my client visits and made me more aware of how God is with me in my work." Camille summarized what many of us felt: "I think it was easier because we were doing it together." Everyone hoped to keep in touch and I offered a final reminder: "Stillness prayer practice is not an end in itself, but a means to becoming more aware, responsive and surrendered to God in every moment of our lives."

## Discussion

- *God's beloved.* Do you find it easy or difficult to accept that you are God's beloved? Why? How do you react to the notion that God is well pleased with you?

- *Stuck.* Where do you struggle to live the prayer "Not my will but yours be done"? What gets in the way of trusting your Creator more fully as a loving parent? How did those wounds of trust develop? What might help you recover confidence in God's care?

- *The teachings of Jesus.* Review the list beginning on page 106. Which of Jesus' instructions about discovering our identity as God's beloved speaks the most to you right now? How or when have you experienced this kind of intimacy with your Creator?

- *Distraction and hurry.* What distracts you from being aware of God's presence? What might help you create more "God space" in your life?

- *Silence, stillness and solitude.* Think of a time you practiced still-ness prayer or solitude. Do you find it easy or difficult to be si-lent and still before God? Do you have a regular practice of prayer that helps you meet with God?

## Exercises

- *Try practicing stillness prayer together* for twenty to thirty minutes.

- *Spend ten minutes writing a prayer* that expresses your longing for intimacy with the Creator (see the poetic prayer at the be-ginning of this chapter for an example [p. 103]). Share your prayers with one another. These prayers can become the "living liturgy" of your family or community.

## Seven-Day Experiments

- *Practice stillness prayer each day* for twenty minutes at a specific time and place.

- *Take a thirty- to ninety-minute solitary walk with God,* using the time to notice your surroundings, reflect or ask God for what you need. Walking can be a powerful way to experience God's presence and beauty revealed in the world around us. And praying while you are moving can create a different mental flow that opens new insights.

- *Write a two-page story* about a critical turning point in your life when you became aware of God's presence and care.

- *Practice the Lord's Table each day at the evening meal for one week.* Celebrating the Lord's Table is an embodied way to consciously recognize the sacrifice of Jesus as our source for life in God's kingdom. The earliest Christians seemed to have practiced this whenever they met in one another's homes as part of sharing a meal together (Acts 2:42-47).

- *Go on a creative adventure.* Spend one to two hours doing something new that feeds your soul and aesthetic vision. Visit a museum or botanical garden. Spend some time at a fabric or art store. Go dancing. Watch a beautiful film or listen to music. Sit in a garden. Buy and prepare a food ingredient you've never cooked before. Or create a song or piece of artwork. The key is to do something novel to help you "taste and see" that God is good.

## Extended Projects and Practices

- *Adopt a weekly prayer practice.* Meet once a week with a person or group to practice stillness prayer or another method of prayer that you find helpful.

- *Keep a journal.* For thirty days write for thirty minutes when you get up each morning. Write whatever comes to your mind without editing. It can be your worry list, the dreams you remember, or prayers about your struggles or hopes for the future. By getting it out onto the page you will become more aware of what is going on in your interior landscape—your true condition—and how God might be trying to speak to you. Meet once a week with a friend or group to check in with what you are noticing as a result of this practice.

- *Organize a silent retreat.* Find a space either in the city or the country that can be borrowed or rented economically—preferably within an hour's drive of where you live. People can share rooms or sleep on floors in common spaces to make it more affordable. Make sure that participants know what the goals and expectations of the retreat are ahead of time. Especially for people who haven't practiced extended solitude before, it helps to have a suggested rhythm and exercises. Work together on simple, healthy meals, like a big pot of soup or stew, salad and bread. You can post a chart and instructions and rotate meal prep and cleanup. Process what you experience at the conclusion of your time. If a whole weekend seems too long or elaborate, start by organizing a four-hour "solo with God" on a Saturday morning. Meet outside at a park (or in a large house if the weather is bad), and afterward gather together to process your experiences over bag lunches.

# 8

# Experiments in Purpose

*The Spirit of the Lord is on me, because he has anointed me to proclaim good news to the poor. He has sent me to proclaim freedom for the prisoners and recovery of sight for the blind, to set the oppressed free, to proclaim the year of the Lord's favor.*

Luke 4:18-19

*For we are God's handiwork, created in Christ Jesus to do good works, which God prepared in advance for us to do.*

Ephesians 2:10

### ABBA, TOGETHER WE GROAN

*You said the reign of love
is like a seed planted deep within
growing like a virus
bringing greater wholeness
making all things new again
But from where we stand
All we can see
Is the dirt where your promises
 lay buried:
We see land scarred by greed,
dark clouds approaching,
We see the wounds and suffering
of women, men and children aching
for a kingdom coming
that can't come soon enough
 Abba, together we groan*

*We are the soil where your promises
 lay hidden
We are the sons and daughters
 of creation
And together we grown in frustration
until the green shoots and ripe fruits
 of your kingdom*

*become as real on earth
as they are in heaven
Awaken our imaginations today
for the reign of love that is more real
than the fears and doubts we feel
Give us courage to name and enjoy
all the gifts the earth reveals.
Lead us to places where our hands
 and our words
can sooth and heal
 Abba, together we groan*

*We wait for sunlight
We pray for rain
We lie awake in the night
with growing pains.*

*Abba, finish the work you began
with the first coming of the chosen one.
finish the work you began
before the creation of our world
 Abba, together we groan*

Mark Scandrette, October 2007

One of the most memorable group experiments I've been a part of happened in a response to a tragedy. Several years ago two of our housemates, Adam and Dan, were on their way to the store when they saw two men arguing with a group of teenagers in the park across the street. Nothing to bother about, they thought, just the normal tension that erupts around the park when people drink too much. But when Adam and Dan returned from the store they found one of the men lying in a pool of blood with a bullet in his head. They quickly dialed 911, but by the time the paramedics arrived it was too late. We later heard the fuller story of what had happened. The man's name was Jesús Estrada, a thirty-two-year-old carpenter who had come into the neighborhood to have the oil changed on his car. As he passed by the park he saw a group of children and teenagers harassing an older gentleman and stepped in to help. After taunting and shouting at Jesús, they fled to the housing projects nearby, and returned with a gun. While trying to be a good Samaritan, Jesús became a target, and left behind a widowed wife and an orphaned five-year-old son. Witnesses said the killers were only ten and twelve years old.

Adam and Dan, obviously shaken, wondered if they could have prevented this tragedy if they had only been willing to step in sooner. As a community we felt prompted to ask, What does it mean to practice the way of Jesus in a neighborhood where people are regularly shot and killed? What could a group of mostly non-native Spanish speakers do to make a difference? We began to brainstorm. Through some initial research we became familiar with the "broken window principle," which suggests that violence occurs in neighborhoods where people get the impression that no one cares—places with high concentrations of graffiti, garbage and broken windows. We decided to create an experiment to address the escalating violence, calling it Barrio Libre, or neighborhood freedom. For eight weeks we gathered as a group each

Wednesday evening to walk the streets praying, picking up trash and greeting neighbors. We called the city to report any graffiti or piles of debris we found. One night we painted mural panels to display as a memorial during Dia de los Muertos, a Mexican holiday honoring lost loved ones. On another night we wrote poetic prayers as we walked and later read them aloud. Here's the poem I wrote, recalling street names where people have been shot in the neighborhood:

> 25th and Shotwell, 25th and Treat, 25th and Portrero
> 24th and Mission, Capp, Shotwell, Folsom, Harrison, York
> Harrison and 24th, Treat and 25th
> Around the corner, down the street, outside my door
> These are the places I can remember off the top of my head
> Where brothers, sons, daughters, sisters
> Were found dead
> Shot down in retaliation drive-bys
> While wearing blue or red
> We hear the sirens
> and we turn our heads
> When the gunshots wake us
> And we rise from our beds
> A mother weeps
> His sister cries
> as the mass is sung
> Before the blood has dried
> In the cracks along these sidewalks
> They say he was a street soldier
> But why couldn't he have been older?
> What revolution, good cause or war did he lose
>         his life for?
> We hear the sirens
> and we turn our heads

When the gunshots wake us
And we rise from our beds
After the candles and trinkets have been swept away
We try to forget about the violence that ruled this day.
But tonight, under these street lights, I will remember
    and pray:
Peace to the immigrant child
Hope to all those in exile
Love to fatherless children
Waiting to be born into the family of the kingdom of love
—Mark Scandrette, October 2006

Working with two friends who were graphic designers, we developed a poster campaign with the slogan "Our Neighborhood: What We Do Matters." Many of our neighbors are new immigrants who, due to the corruption in their homelands, are afraid or reluctant to call the police if they see danger. These families also have to work two or three jobs in order to make ends meet and don't have time to advocate for neighborhood safety. With our Barrio Libre campaign we wanted to communicate a vision of ownership, pride and respect—that our neighborhood could be a clean and welcoming place where children and older people can walk down the streets without fear. The posters, written in Spanish and English, showed pictures of three behaviors that were hurting the neighborhood: a person going to the bathroom on the sidewalk, someone throwing trash on the ground and a hand pointing a gun. These images were crossed out and below were pictures of the alternatives: someone using a toilet, a hand putting trash in a garbage can and two people shaking hands.

We put the posters up around the neighborhood and asked local businesses to display them in their storefronts. The response to our project was overwhelming. Schoolteachers called requesting stacks of posters to send home with their students. A feature story was written about us for a major regional newspaper. Our posters became so popular that we even started seeing photocopies of them displayed in businesses in other districts. With hundreds of people joining our efforts, we've seen slow but steady improvements in the neighborhood. Barrio Libre made us realize how much impact a small group of people can have when they work together and get creative. And it galvanized our sense of common work as we took steps to enact our purposes as agents of God's healing.

I was hanging Barrio Libre posters outside a public housing project recently with my friend Nathan when a nine-year-old girl approached me on the sidewalk and asked, "Whatcha doing?" I explained our dream for a safer neighborhood. "There were gunshots outside my house at midnight last night," she said matter-of-factly. As I told her how sorry I was, she said, "You can put them posters up, but somebody's just goin' to tear them down."

"We'll just have to keep working together to love the neighborhood until it gets better," I said. We said goodbye and began moving down the block, when she called after us, "You be safe now."

From street violence to ecological destruction to global poverty and warfare, we are clearly in the midst of a great struggle to see God's shalom become manifest on earth as it is in heaven. An apprentice to Jesus learns to make the realization of God's creative and restoring work their core purpose.

At the beginning of his public life Jesus went into the synagogue and announced his purpose: to proclaim good news to the poor, freedom to those held captive and sight for the blind, and to release the oppressed and proclaim the year of God's favor on all people (Luke 4:18-19). Everywhere he went, Jesus brought God's shalom by welcoming outcast and forgotten people, proclaiming good news to those in suffering, healing people from sickness and making the oppressed well. And now we also are invited to discover our purpose as agents of God's healing and restoring work.

## A Vision for Enacting Our Purpose as Agents of God's Healing: Why Are We Here?

Look! All around us the Creator is at work liberating and restoring what is broken and inviting all people to return to their source. You and I were made to find our deepest joy and greatest satisfaction, not from doing whatever we want, but by surrendering to God's will. We are the light this world needs. We are agents of God's healing, justice and love—especially for the poor and weak and those who suffer. We don't have to be concerned about becoming the greatest or getting credit. The Father sees and knows the good work we do to love and serve. Ask for God's reign to come to every place and person in your path and expect to see freedom multiplied. This is why we are invited to live and pray the words: "Your kingdom come, your will be done, on earth as it is in heaven."

## What Jesus Instructs Us to Be and Do to Fulfill Our Purpose

- *Make the realization of God's dreams your highest priority:* "But seek first [God's] kingdom and [God's] righteousness" (Matthew 6:33).

- *Expect God's activity and pray that more liberators will be sent:* "The harvest is plentiful but the workers are few. Ask the Lord of the harvest, therefore, to send out workers into his harvest field" (Matthew 9:37-38).

- *Serve with humility and don't seek special titles or status:* "Whoever wants to become great among you must be your servant, and whoever wants to be first must be slave of all" (Mark 10:43-44). "But you are not to be called 'Rabbi,' for you have only one Master and you are all brothers. And do not call anyone on earth 'father,' for you have one Father, and he is in heaven. Nor are you to be called 'teacher,' for you have one Teacher, the Messiah. The greatest among you will be your servant. For those who exalt themselves will be humbled, and those who humble themselves will be exalted" (Matthew 23:8-12).

- *Pray:* "Your kingdom come, your will be done" (Matthew 6:10).

- *Let your life shine:* "Let your light shine before others, that they may see your good deeds and glorify your Father in heaven" (Matthew 5:16).

- *Welcome and include the forgotten and care for "the least of these"—the hungry, thirsty, naked, sick and lonely:* "But when you give a banquet, invite the poor, the crippled, the lame, the blind, and you will be blessed. Although they cannot repay you, you will be repaid at the resurrection of the righteous" (Luke 14:13-14). "For I was hungry and you gave me something to eat, I was thirsty and you gave me something to drink, I was a stranger and you invited me in, I needed clothes and you clothed me, I was sick and you looked after me, I was in prison and you came to visit me" (Matthew 25:35-36).

- *Be secretive about your good deeds:* "Be careful not to do your 'acts of righteousness' in front of others, to be seen by them" (Matthew 6:1).

- *Make disciples by practicing and teaching the Way:* "Go and make disciples of all nations, baptizing them in the name of the Father and of the Son and of the Holy Spirit, and teaching them to obey everything I have commanded you" (Matthew 28:18-20).

## Expect Opportunity

*Be very careful, then, how you live—not as unwise but as wise, making the most of every opportunity.*

Ephesians 5:15-16

If you are like me, you may want to be available to care for those who are hungry, thirsty, naked, sick or lonely, but sometimes the current demands of life make it difficult to find the time. One day as I looked over my schedule I became frustrated and prayed, "God, you see that I don't have space in my calendar, but I still want to be part of your healing work today. Please bring someone into my path that needs your help." At noon I had a lunch appointment, and while we talked over tamales we heard a scream outside the restaurant. A woman had just gone into a seizure, fallen violently to the ground and split her jaw wide open on the sidewalk. Her friends were hysterical and overwhelmed. I quickly ran outside, bent over and cradled the woman's head in my arms as I dialed an emergency number. Within a few minutes the paramedics arrived and were able to stabilize her. As they loaded the woman into an ambulance her friends kept exclaiming, "Oh, you are an angel—you saved her life!" I quietly went back into the restaurant and sat down. My companion looked stunned and said, "I've never seen anything like that before—I'm amazed by how quickly you responded." Then she began to cry, explaining that the incident reminded her of the recent death of her father, brother and uncle in a tragic accident. We spent the rest of our working lunch talking through how she was navigating her pain and loss. I left the restaurant smiling when I realized that the events of the past hour corresponded directly with what I had prayed that morning.

## Resonate

Sometimes a dramatic new experience can change your perspective on where you live and the people you see every day. Karen was from a semirural area on the outskirts of the San Francisco Bay. With some apprehension, she came into the city for a daylong intensive called Resonate. She pushed herself because she wanted to get a broader perspective on God's heart for people. During the orientation, as the group sat atop a rocky bluff overlooking San Francisco, she kept thinking about how different this was from where she lived. Their assignment for the day was to walk a prescribed route through three different neighborhoods, exploring as many new places as possible. The facilitator said, "In the familiar routines of life it's easy to become blind to the needs of the people around us. The structures of our society also tend to segment us by districts and social classes, so that we have limited exposure to people who are different from us. Today we want you to wander into places you might not normally go and meet new people. Be curious. Ask questions, and listen."

Karen started looking over the maps provided, hoping that she wouldn't get lost, as the facilitator continued, "There are three ways of prayer we want you to practice today. The first is inspired by the words of the apostle Paul: 'God, show me where your glory is displayed in this place and among these people.' God's eternal power and divine nature are revealed in what we can see all around us. Look for God's glory today in the beauty of the trees and flowers, in architecture, food and fashion, and in the faces of the people you meet. In fact, as a fun part of this exercise we want you to taste at least five new foods today. The second prayer is, 'God, help me to think your thoughts and feel your feelings for the people and places that I see.' Saying this prayer helps us acknowledge that we don't always see as God sees. A third way we want you to pray is, 'May your kingdom come and your will be done here and now as it is in heaven.' When you notice things that break your heart, ask for God's dreams to be restored." A final instruction was to take a break partway through the day at a park or café, and write a poetic prayer inspired by one of the three prayers presented.

Karen paired up with two high school students and they quickly made their way down into the first neighborhood, past graffiti-tagged walls and alleyways painted with colorful murals. When she walked by a homeless person pushing a grocery cart she had the courage to stop and say hello. As they explored the shops along the boulevard they tasted pastries from a Mexican panaderia, exotic tropical fruits from a bodega and tacos made with beef brains. They made fast friends at a Filipino restaurant by trying balut, a fertilized and fermented duck egg widely considered a delicacy. They also visited a psychedelic head shop and a Buddhist monastery where an eager guide gave them a tour of the temple and answered their questions. Many things that Karen saw were different from home, while others, like the migrants waiting for work on street corners, were all too familiar—except that she was learning to see them in a new way, with eyes of compassion.

Karen felt particularly out of place as she walked through a historic gay district of the city—a culture and people largely unfamiliar to her. As she concentrated on praying "God, help me think your thoughts and feel your feelings," she realized that she had never really considered how God feels about those among us who are gay, lesbian, bisexual or transgendered. Sexual orientation, in her experience, had been a moral and political issue to debate. But now, as she prayed, sitting in a corner café in the heart of the district, she saw *people*—people she knew God loves. She reflected on this insight while trying to write her poetic prayer and something clicked. She remembered a person back home who rode horses at the same stable where she was a member. Though she chatted regularly with other people around the stables, it never occurred to her to even say hello to this woman whom she presumed was in a same-sex relationship. When she returned home, she resolved to be more openhearted. Gradually the two women became friends, and over time, Karen was instrumental in helping her new friend rediscover a relationship with God. She even became part of Karen's faith community. How did this happen? It began with an experiment. Karen's heart first needed to be changed so that she could be a channel of God's restoring work in her friend's life.

## Crossing Boundaries of Class and Culture

The issues and characteristics that once distinguished cities from suburbs and suburbs from small towns are dramatically shifting or dissolving. In many places the suburb is rapidly becoming the new inner city, as urban centers become more desirable to the upwardly mobile. This makes for interesting new cultural mashups, like Halal markets in Midwestern farm towns or Latin barrios emerging in once tony suburbs. At one time, crossing an ethnic or cultural boundary required a plane ticket and a passport. Now, for many of us it simply means walking out the front door of our house or peeking into the next cubicle at the office. This brings up exciting new challenges and opportunities for people seeking to practice the way of Jesus.

I know of a Chinese-language church that began when new immigrants were only allowed to settle in one area of a growing suburb. Since that time, most members of the congregation have moved to other areas, and the neighborhood, later populated by Spanish-speaking immigrants, has become at-risk with violence and drug activity. The congregation began to wonder how they could reach out to their new neighbors who were so different from them culturally and socioeconomically. People from the church decided to try an experiment. For eight weeks they walked the neighborhood, meeting neighbors, offering prayer and discovering needs. Imagine the beauty of this unlikely scene: a group of well-heeled, older Chinese folks talking and praying with their Latin neighbors with mariachi music blaring from a lowrider's stereo in the background. They were surprised by the warm reception they received, and learned that despite their culture and language differences, they had a shared reverence for Christ. The congregation started a tutoring program for children in the neighborhood and continues to ask deeper questions about how they can leverage their resources to address needs.

## Feasting with the Forgotten

Jesus once said, "When you give a banquet, invite the poor, the crippled, the lame, the blind, and you will be blessed" (Luke 14:13-14). Most towns and cities have places where the poor and homeless gather—a public park, abandoned industrial area or soup kitchen on skid row. These are brothers and sisters, mothers and fathers, sons and daughters who, for a variety of circumstances, find themselves isolated and alone. You can find similarly lonely or forgotten people in our prisons, jails, public hospitals and nursing homes. Our society tends to segment those of us who have and those who do not. Yet something magical happens when the rich and the poor eat together. When we do, we live the parable and celebrate the signs of a kingdom coming that is already here.

We like to help organize "feasts of friendship" with our poor and homeless neighbors. In our city, it's not uncommon for people to drive by encampments of homeless people, dumping off food or bags of clothes. What we hope to offer is something more than one-way charity—friendship between people who can each benefit from knowing one another. We once did a group experiment where for seven weeks we cooked and ate dinner with an encampment of folks living underneath the freeway underpass near our neighborhood. Our friend Tom, who hadn't been around homeless or addicted people much, expressed some apprehension about going under the bridge to eat with strangers in the dark. He demonstrated a lot of courage simply by showing up, and his fear gradually subsided as we all cooked and ate and played games together. It was surprisingly easy to strike up conversations and people shared deeply about the triumphs and tragedies in their lives.

On the last week of the experiment we threw a big party, complete with a turkey dinner, decorations, a piñata and battery-operated Christmas lights. We had many laughs trying to get the candy and hygiene supplies to spill from the piñata. Tom, who volunteered to be the DJ for the party, brought a portable sound system and played a mix of music that kept everyone dancing all night. Over the seven weeks of the experiment, Tom had taken significant steps toward overcoming his fears, and had become more comfortable relating to people who struggle with problems different than his own. He was even concerned about what would happen to the friendships he'd started and resolved to make time for the homeless people he saw on a regular basis in his own neighborhood.

## Discerning Your Life Purpose

Taking small risks to love and serve can spur deeper questions about life purpose. My friend Damon once went on a trip to an orphanage in Ethiopia that "wrecked" him for normal life. "I spend the best hours of my day making the world go faster," he said of his work at a technology company. He had followed the script that he'd been given as a boy: go to school, get an advanced degree, work for a good company that pays well and save aggressively for retirement. "I'm not sure that's what I want my life to be about anymore—or how that fits with the reality and opportunities of God's kingdom," he said. After reflecting on deeper questions of vision and purpose, he ventured into a careful process of reinvention—deciding that rather than making an abrupt change he would adopt intentional practices to lean into his new vision. With a small group of friends he committed to spending an hour each day in study, prayer and reflection. One evening a week they volunteered together at an AIDS hospice where they would care for the needs of dying people until late at night. Eventually his passion for activities outside of work made him wonder if he actually needed to work full time. As an experiment he lived on a smaller portion of his income and saved or gave the rest away. He was surprised by how much less he needed to live if he avoided weekend splurges and eating out. Eventually he decided to limit his working hours and told his supervisor that he would be leaving each day at 5:00 p.m. A few weeks later he was promoted to team manager because his supervisor noticed that he was more focused and productive than the other people. Eventually, Damon began working part time so he could spend more of his energy serving. Today he is married with two children, supports his family by working full time again and is active in the Chinese-speaking immigrant community where he lives. Through small, intentional shifts Damon was able to discern a rhythm of life that allows him to live out of a deeper purpose.

We are each being invited to discern how to live out of our deeper purpose as agents of God's healing work in our world.

## Discussion

- *Barrio Libre.* As you think about your local context, what are the most immediate struggles for God's shalom to be established?

- *The least of these.* In your local context, who are the people who are hungry, thirsty, naked, sick or lonely? Where do they live? Where would you have the opportunity to regularly rub shoulders with the least among us? Now consider the same questions from a global perspective.

- *The teachings of Jesus.* Review the list beginning on page 128. Which of Jesus' instructions about enacting our purpose speaks the most to you right now? Why?

- *Expect opportunity.* Recall a time you had an unexpected opportunity to help someone in a crisis or emergency. How did you respond? How did it make you feel? What distracts you from being open to healing opportunities?

- *Resonate.* What types of people do you stereotype or struggle to see as God's beloved?

- *Cultural boundaries.* What are the class or cultural boundaries that exist in your city? How can you be intentional about crossing those boundaries in love?

## Exercises

- *Complete the life purpose survey* included in the appendix (see page 196) and discuss your responses.

- *Spend ten minutes writing a poetic prayer* about how you long to see God's kingdom come to your neighborhood or city. Read your poetic prayers to one another.

## Seven-Day Experiments

- *Seeing as God sees.* Make a commitment for one week to look into the eyes of each person you meet, pausing to see them as God's beloved, your sister or brother, and a person of priceless worth and dignity.

- *Expect opportunity.* Each morning for a week, ask God for the opportunity to be an agent of healing.

- *Eat with the lonely.* Along with a friend, eat at a local soup kitchen or visit a hospital, prison or nursing home.

- *Resonate.* Along with a friend, go on a two- or three-hour "resonate" walk similar to the one described in this chapter. Choose a high-population, foot-traffic neighborhood, ideally with a mix of residences and businesses, in an area of your town or city where you can cross a boundary of class and culture. Explore as many businesses and public gathering spaces as possible. Taste at least three things you've never had before, purchased from local vendors (not franchise restaurants, if possible). Ask questions of people you encounter, and listen to their answers. Pray one of these prayers as you walk:
  - Show me where your glory is displayed in this place and among these people.
  - Help me to think your thoughts and feel your feelings for the people and places that I see.
  - May your kingdom come and your will be done here and now as it is in heaven.

## Extended Projects and Practices

- *Feast with the forgotten.* Live the parable (Luke 14:13-14) by organizing a special dinner or series of dinners with people who are usually left out. You might find it helpful to coordinate with a local homeless shelter or other agency.

- *Initiate a compassion or justice project.* Do some research to identify a critical need in your area, and organize a six- to eight-week group project to address that need through service and advocacy.

- *Announce the good news of the kingdom.* Read the instructions Jesus gave to his earliest disciples in Matthew 10. Brainstorm how you might create a provocative public campaign that invites people into the good news of God's kingdom. What language and approach would effectively communicate with people where you live? How can you engage in a way that creates interest and surprise? Public art? Performance? Free services (such as haircuts and massages)? Public offers of prayer for healing? Be creative and try out your best ideas.

# 9

# Experiments in Security

*For where your treasure is, there your heart will be also.*

Luke 12:34

*The universe produces all that is
needed:
Food and Fabrics,
Water and Wood,
Bricks and Clay,
Sunshine and Rain.
The Maker brings these to us as a gift
each day
—knowing that we are happiest
when we live close to the soil
aware of our source
consciously embracing all things
with thanks.*

*The secret is that we are fabulously
wealthy
Living like Kings and Queens
In a garden of leisure and luxury.
What we have is enough . . . and more
If we lack anything, it is the*

*simple pleasure
To enjoy what we already possess
Though so often we find ourselves
chasing after joyless schemes and
business
denying our inheritance
And wanting what can only make us
choked, tired and desperate.*

*Today, let us find goodness
In the small things
Tasting the abundance you have
lavished on us
With eager open hands
Giving and receiving
Trusting and Completing
the circle that began
With the gift of life*

Mark Scandrette, 2007

When Damon and I met at the Woodside Café to prepare for an upcoming simplicity workshop, we were quite conscious of the irony. In a quaint little town that is home to movie stars and technology moguls, this café is regarded as the place where billion-dollar deals are pitched over coffee and pastries.

"The collective net worth of everyone in this place dropped significantly when we walked in," quipped Damon as we searched for a table.

I laughed. "True—most people here have more financial wealth than you or I ever will, but there is a lot more to God's abundance than houses, money and stock options. What if we measured wealth in purposeful work, simple pleasures and meaningful relationships?"

Overhearing us, a well-cultivated, middle-aged woman at the next table interjected, "You're onto something. I'm living alone in a multimillion dollar home and my teenage daughter is on drugs and dating a man wanted for murder. I'd give anything to have a better relationship with my daughter—and to see her making better choices."

Even as we seek to live in an economy that mirrors God's reign of abundance, it is hard to shed our sense of scarcity. Despite the vision of the kingdom of love, we are easily tempted to maintain a materialist view of who is well-off and what constitutes true wealth.

Yet there are those moments that challenge our paradigms. I once stood in a mud-floor shanty in El Salvador, my hand in the hand of a mother who feeds her family of eight on two dollars a day. I can still hear her whispered prayer of thanks. Her ability to see abundance in poverty both instructs and haunts me.

After traveling on several occasions to the developing world, Melissa felt a weight of responsibility for making less consumptive choices. It was painfully ironic to her that she struggled with overeating while so many people on the planet barely have enough. As an experiment she decided to live for forty days on a dollar a day (aside from rent and utilities)—the amount that many families in the developing world have to live on. This would help her address her dependency on the pleasure and comfort of food, help her live in some measure of solidarity with the struggles of the poorest people in the world, and allow her to give what she saved to people who are truly hungry. With remarkable tenacity and discipline, Melissa stuck to her commitment and kept a daily journal of what she learned and experienced about simplicity, contentment and gratitude.

Perhaps the huge disparities of wealth in our world are precisely why money, like sexuality, is one of those things we find easier to discuss in theoretical rather than practical terms. Money is one of the most difficult topics of conversation we have in our community. Take Kevin, one of the most vocal about his disdain for consumerism, corporate greed and the evils of "the Man." He wears the same thrift-store clothes every day. He and his wife, Rebecca, spent most of their twenties as activists, traveling and volunteering in developing countries. When we decided as a community to disclose what we earn and spend and how much we owe or save, Kevin and Rebecca expressed both trepidation and excitement.

At their turn, Kevin held up a crumpled piece of paper. "This is the first time we've ever created a budget. I guess we've been scared to see our true situation. Basically, we are spending a thousand dollars more a month than we earn. At our current rate of payment, it will take us twenty-five years to pay off our student loans and consumer debts. I feel so dumb. I wish someone had taught me how to handle money earlier in life."

Rebecca chimed in, "You know we have a little one on the way. Someday we'd like to buy a home, and we hope to keep pursuing our dreams and ideals—but I don't see how that is possible now. I wonder if we should both just go out and get corporate jobs."

Audrey, a woman who left college to deal with a childhood

trauma, told us that her full-time service job (beginning every day at 4:00 a.m.) was only providing her enough money to pay rent with little left over for food. "When I have unanticipated expenses, I've been putting them on my credit card. I eventually want to go back to school, but I don't know how I ever will," she said.

Jennifer, an M.B.A. working as a finance director, spoke last. "I'm hesitant to share because my situation is so different from many others. I've been trying to live simply for a long time. I don't have any debts. I make six figures, and after maxing out my 401k and contributing 35 percent of my income to church and charity, I still have thousands of dollars left each month that I'm not sure what to do with."

As a community we disclose our spending and earning as a means of discerning what the Spirit is inviting us into with our finances. It became clear that seeking the way of Jesus with our resources requires a different prescription for each of us. Some of us needed to curb our spending and deal with debts or consumptive habits. Some of us needed financial help and prayer for better-paying work. And some of us needed to get more creative and daring about spending and sharing the resources God had given us.

Over the next few months we supported each other through various transitions. Audrey moved in with a family to save up for school. Kevin and Rebecca made a commitment to pay down their debts over the next three years by taking on more work and learning to control their spending. We encouraged Jennifer to add a little pleasure and celebration to her ascetic life. Being vulnerable with each other about our finances didn't feel legalistic because we approached it with a sense of playfulness, and an understanding that we were each being invited to take our next step toward living in God's abundance.

It is essential that we seek to live toward that abundance, for the practice of simplicity by itself has a significant shadow side.

When we begin to judge others by the voluntary choices we've made, or when we make an idol of our own resourcefulness, simplicity ceases to give life and becomes a divisive burden.

Over the years I've prided myself in being radically frugal, fastidious with budgets and careful with spending. I've mastered the art of thrift-store shopping and the dumpster dive. But when I'm honest, I'm able to admit that my reluctance to spend money hasn't made me more content or generous. In fact, it's only made me a more shrewd materialist—a guy with a fetish for the great deal, who gets his fix by getting things for free or on the cheap. You don't need money to be obsessive or materialistic. An apprentice of Jesus learns to rely on the resources God provides.

## Twelve Baskets of Bread Left Over: How Jesus Lived in the Security of God's Abundance

In the life of Jesus, an image that epitomizes his sense of abundance is the miraculous feeding of the multitude. Jesus had just found out that his friend John the Baptist had been beheaded and his disciples were returning, physically and emotionally exhausted from their work. Suddenly, an unexpected crowd of thousands gathered, desperate for guidance and healing. When the disciples pleaded with Jesus to dismiss the crowd he offered up a challenge, saying, "You give them something to eat." He then proceeded to give thanks over a few loaves of bread and fish that suddenly multiplied to feed everyone, leaving twelve baskets of food left over. When it seems like our physical and emotional resources are spent, there is always a source for more. Abundance comes from being open-handed to give and receive, trusting that the Father always provides what is needed.

Jesus was at home in the Father's world, whether housed or

homeless, eating at a feast or gleaning from the edges of a field. With a whip he drove currency traders, along with their sheep and cattle, out of the temple, turning over their tables and scattering their money. "People do not live by bread alone," he countered to the devil, and when his disciples once asked why he wasn't eating he replied, "I have food to eat that you know nothing about. . . . My food is to do the will of him who sent me" (John 4:32, 34).

In a culture that places particular value on economic and material prosperity, instant gratification, debt-based economic growth and rapid economic progress motivated by a sense of scarcity and irrational fears about economic security, we are being invited to be intentional about living out a vision of God's abundance and generosity. If we don't make conscious choices about our relationship to money and possessions, the forces of a dominant culture will tend to make those choices for us. By first dealing with our heart motivations about money and possessions, the practical details of how we manage our resources are navigated more easily. We start from where we are to live into the greater wholeness of God's kingdom. If we feel discouraged or trapped by our current financial situation, the invitation is to simply discern how to take the next step toward abundance, gratefulness, contentment, generosity, sustainability and trust.

## The Vision for Embracing Security: How Can We Thrive?

We are sustained through God's abundance. The Creator delights in giving us what we ask for. We don't have to be greedy because the resources we need will always be provided. We can share what we have and what we receive. We don't have to worry or be afraid of anything, including what will happen in the future. We don't have to be jealous of people who hoard things, thinking that we live only by what we can see. Knowing where true provision comes from, we are free to live generously with content and grateful hearts. This is why we are invited to live and pray the words: "Give us this day our daily bread."

## What Jesus Instructs Us to Be and Do to Discover True Security

- *Trust and do not be afraid:* "Do not let your hearts be troubled and do not be afraid" (John 14:27).

- *Do not worry or be anxious about anything—food, clothes, survival or the future:* "Do not worry about your life" (Matthew 6:25).

- *Ask God for whatever you need:* "Ask and it will be given to you; seek and you will find; knock and the door will be opened to you" (Luke 11:9).

- *Be generous:* "Sell your possessions and give to the poor" (Luke 12:33).

- *Give discretely and privately:* "When you give to the needy, do not let your left hand know what your right hand is doing" (Matthew 6:3).

- *Use your resources to make friends:* "Use worldly wealth to gain friends for yourselves" (Luke 16:9).

- *Do not be greedy:* "Watch out! Be on your guard against all kinds of greed; life does not consist in an abundance of possessions" (Luke 12:15).

- *Do not hoard money or possessions:* "Do not store up for yourselves treasures on earth, where moth and rust destroy, and where thieves break in and steal" (Matthew 6:19).

- *Make God's kingdom your treasure instead of material wealth:* "Store up for yourselves treasures in heaven, where moth and rust do not destroy, and where thieves do not break in and steal" (Matthew 6:20).

- *Pay your taxes but don't rely on government solutions:* "Give back to Caesar what is Caesar's and to God what is God's" (Mark 12:17).

It was night in Tijuana, and I was sitting in a shanty apartment with twenty-five students. Outside, trucks full of soldiers with mounted machine guns patrolled the restless streets, attempting to keep order amidst the drug cartel wars. These students were participating in a five-month discipleship training school at which I was teaching. Most were from the northern provinces of Mexico. That night, an unexpected guest joined our discussion—a young man from across the border in San Diego. At a question-and-answer session, our visitor spoke first: "I've been reading a book that has convinced me that as Christians we are all called to poverty. Do you agree?"

I watched bewilderment and confusion spread over the faces of my students. "You've picked an interesting place to ask this question," I commented. "Let's hear what your Mexican brothers and sisters have to say."

Roberto responded first. "I don't understand. How can God call us to poverty when we were born poor?"

"If you can choose to be poor, then you aren't really poor," added Luisa.

We soon came up with a list of what both the rich and poor can learn from Jesus' teachings on material possessions. Then, after an hour of lively discussion, we surmised that perhaps we aren't all called to poverty but are invited instead to live into the reality of God's reign with simplicity of purpose, gratefulness of heart, radical contentment, ruthless trust and willing generosity—qualities that a person can pursue from within any economic situation. Together we have been given the reign of God and are being invited into risky generosity—leveraging our time, money, talents and resources for the good of the world.

## Discussion

- *True wealth.* How do you think wealth is measured differently in the economy of God's kingdom?

- *Sharing budgets.* Does the prospect of sharing how much you earn and spend with a group of people sound exciting or scary? Why? What might be a benefit of such a practice?

- *Twelve baskets of food left over.* Describe an experience you've had of God's abundance.

- *The teachings of Jesus.* Which one of the instructions Jesus gave about security (see list on page 145) speaks the most to you right now?

- *Worries and fears.* Where do you struggle to trust in the security that God promises? What makes you worried or afraid?

- *Money and possessions.* What do you struggle with the most when it comes to money and possessions? What would help you in those struggles?

- *Global need.* How are we to see God's abundance in light of the poverty and economic injustices in our world? What are the responsibilities of people who benefit from the inequitable distribution of resources globally? What would it look like for you to adopt a lifestyle of voluntary simplicity?

## Exercises

- *Work through the gratitude and contentment survey* included in the appendix (see page 198).

- *As a group, create a list of resources* you are willing to share with each other, including possessions different group members own and distinct knowledge and skills that each person could contribute to the group.

## Seven-Day Experiments

- *Gratitude.* Keep a gratitude log for one week. Write down ten things each day (without repeating anything) that you are grateful for. Share your gratitude log with one another the following week.

- *Time/money journal.* To become more aware of how you are utilizing your resources, keep a detailed journal of where you spend your time and money.

- *Sabbath keeping.* Taking a day of rest is a way of expressing faith in what God provides. What does a deeply regenerative day look like for you? How would you feast and celebrate what God has given you? What would you abstain from to pursue deeper rest? Answer these questions for yourself and schedule (and take) a Sabbath day.

- *Worries and fears.* Each morning make a list of the worries and fears that go through your head, and surrender them to God.

- *Simplify.* Make a radical change in how you spend money for seven days (e.g., restrict your food budget to two dollars a day, or give up morning coffee or eating out). Collect the money you save and donate it toward global poverty relief.

- *Celebrate abundance.* Finding security in God's abundance implies both radical contentment and generous celebration. Jesus fed the hungry crowds and turned water into more wine than anyone could drink at a wedding! This week, plan, budget for and deliver a lavish gift or special feast for your friends or family.

- *Buy fair trade and local.* We are conditioned to expect to get things as cheaply as possible, which often means unsafe working conditions or underpayment to workers, or environmental damage. We vote for the kind of future we want by how we spend our resources. Do you know whether the goods you buy are sourced equitably? This week experiment with only buying local and fairly sourced goods.

## Extended Projects and Practices

- *Have2Give1*. Invite a group of friends to join you in redistributing resources and possessions for a month (see chapter one for an example).

- *Collect and give away resources.* As a group, pool a certain percentage of your incomes and, by consensus, decide how you will spend the money to bless others.

- *Budgets and financial planning.* Over several weeks, develop personal financial goals, create budgets and share what you earn and spend with the group.

- *Voluntary simplicity.* Organize a group of friends to embark on a three-month experiment in voluntary simplicity. Make a commitment not to buy any consumer goods (e.g., clothes, books or music, household electronics or appliances), or decide not to add any new calendar commitments.

# 10

# Experiments in Community

*My command is this: Love each other as I have loved you. Greater love has no one than this: to lay down one's life for one's friends.*

John 15:12-13

*In [Christ] you . . . are being built together to become a dwelling in which God lives by his Spirit.*

Ephesians 2:22

As I write, I'm flipping through pictures from our first intentional community vow ceremony six years ago. On a beautiful afternoon, among crowds of Sunday picnickers and sunbathers, we gathered on a grassy hillside at a park overlooking the city. Fifty of us sat on blankets while a few of us took turns offering songs, poems and reflections on the yearlong vows we were taking to live out the teachings of Jesus together. I can see the eager smiles on the faces in the photos, aglow with the soft light of the setting sun. It was an occasion that had the anticipation and rare mix of guests you might expect at a wedding party. Many of our parents, siblings and friends were on hand to bear witness to the promises we were making. At the conclusion of the ceremony, we celebrated the Lord's Supper with a toast and shared a lovely table spread with flowers, homemade foods and bottles of wine. Lingering in the park until long after dark, we joked, laughed and played music together as a cool fog settled over the skyline.

Complex emotions surface now as I look back at these photos, seeing the faces of old friends and calling to mind the many adventures we've had—the cross-country road trips, hot-spring dips, dance parties and hours spent cooking, welcoming strangers or picking up trash. I remember our shared joys and triumphs, tears and tensions, and late nights up asking questions or praying for answers. We put much energy into helping each other through the crises of lost loves, a lost job and shattered dreams.

I notice that my beard was less speckled with gray back then and that most of us now wear different hairstyles or clothes. And our children are much taller now. Babies born since then have learned to walk and talk and run. Some people have moved on or moved away. Marriages and partnerships have ended or begun. Over many seasons we've worked to give birth to one another's dreams and mourned each other's losses. We've been embraced, cared for, cherished and misunderstood. We've argued, fought and forgiven. We've risked loving and being loved, hurting and being hurt, knowing and being known.

Life in community reveals who we really are. We bring our best and worst to our relationships with one another. Our sense of belonging is where we may feel the most wounded and where the gospel of Jesus offers us the greatest hope. Jesus modeled and promised a revolutionary way of love that could transform our relationships at every level. The vision of belonging that Jesus embodied and taught calls us to a love that is far more ruthless and tender than seems humanly possible. It is a kind of love that can empower you to treat your worst enemy as your dearest friend and to keep hanging on, forgiving, believing and hoping against hope for love to win. An apprentice of Jesus learns to love as God loves.

## Washing the Feet of the Disciples: How Jesus Modeled True Community

The image from the life of Jesus that perhaps best captures the love we are made to give and receive is the episode when he washed his disciples' feet. It was on the evening of his arrest. Knowing that Judas would betray him and that the others would soon deny or abandon him, Jesus got up from the table, took off his robes, picked up a basin and towel and began to wash their dirty feet. Picture the Messiah kneeling before Judas, gently drying his toes with a towel; John the disciple said that at that moment he showed the full extent of his love—to the very end (John 13:1).

### The Vision for a Life of Belonging: How Can We Belong?

You and I are infinitely loved, having received an eternal source of love to share. We are forgiven, and are empowered to forgive whenever we are wronged. Broken relationships can be mended. We can live at peace with one another. Love frees us to live without anger, bitterness, lust or judgment. We can be authentic and honest with each other and keep our promises. We can love and bless people who take advantage of us or even hate us—because love wins over all. This is why we are invited to live and pray the words: "Forgive us our debts as we also have forgiven our debtors."

### What Jesus Instructs Us to Be and Do in Order to Experience True Community

As you read through these instructions, keep in mind that they apply not only to the people we would choose as our companions, but also to the whole ecology of our relationships, including our extended families, coworkers, neighbors, strangers and enemies.

• *Love one another and do to others what you would have them do to you:* "Love one another" (John 13:34). "So in everything, do to others what you would have them do to you" (Matthew 7:12).

- *Serve one another:* "Now that I, your Lord and Teacher, have washed your feet, you also should wash one another's feet. I have set you an example that you should do as I have done for you" (John 13:14-15).

- *Forgive tenaciously:* "If you hold anything against anyone, forgive them, so that your Father in heaven may forgive you your sins" (Mark 11:25).

- *Overcome anger:* "You have heard that it was said to the people long ago, 'You shall not murder, and anyone who murders will be subject to judgment.' But I tell you that anyone who is angry with a brother or sister will be subject to judgment. Again, anyone who says to a brother or sister, 'Raca,' is answerable to the Sanhedrin. And anyone who says, 'You fool!' will be in danger of the fire of hell" (Matthew 5:21-22).

- *Do not judge—but exercise discernment about who you trust:* "Do not judge, or you too will be judged. . . . Do not give dogs what is sacred; do not throw your pearls to pigs. If you do, they may trample them under their feet, and then turn and tear you to pieces" (Matthew 7:1, 6).

- *Seek reconciliation with the people you have wronged:* "Have salt in yourselves, and be at peace with each other" (Mark 9:50). "Therefore, if you are offering your gift at the altar and there remember that your brother or sister has something against you, leave your gift there in front of the altar. First go and be reconciled to that person; then come and offer your gift" (Matthew 5:23-24).

- *Deal directly with the person who has wronged you:* "If a brother or sister sins, go and point out the fault, just between the two of you. If they listen to you, you have won them over. But if they will not listen, take one or two others along, so that 'every matter may be established by the testimony of two or three witnesses.' If they still refuse to listen, tell it to the church; and if they refuse to listen even to the church, treat them as you would a pagan or a tax collector" (Matthew 18:15-17).

- *Keep your promises and commitments:* "You have heard that it was said, 'You shall not commit adultery.' But I tell you that anyone who looks at a woman lustfully has already committed adultery with her in his heart. . . . It has been said, 'Anyone who divorces his wife must give her a certificate of divorce.' But I tell you that anyone who divorces his wife, except for sexual immorality, causes her to become an adulteress, and anyone who marries the divorced woman commits adultery. Again, you have heard that it was said to the people long ago, 'Do not break your oath, but fulfill to the Lord the vows you have made.' But I tell you, do not swear an oath at all: either by heaven, for it is God's throne; or by the earth, for it is his footstool; or by Jerusalem, for it is the city of the Great King. And do not swear by your head, for you cannot make even one hair white or black. All you need to say is simply 'Yes,' or 'No'; anything beyond this comes from the evil one" (Matthew 5:27-37).

- *Love your enemies and bless those who curse you:* "But to you who are listening I say: Love your enemies, do good to those who hate you, bless those who curse you, pray for those who mistreat you. If someone slaps you on one cheek, turn the other also. If someone takes your coat, do not withhold your shirt. Give to everyone who asks you, and if anyone takes what belongs to you, do not demand it back" (Luke 6:27-30).

- *Welcome children and consider how your decisions will affect future generations:* "Whoever welcomes one of these little children in my name welcomes me; and whoever welcomes me does not welcome me but the one who sent me" (Mark 9:37). "Things that cause people to stumble are bound to come, but woe to anyone through whom they come. It would be better for you to be thrown into the sea with a millstone tied around your neck than for you to cause one of these little ones to stumble. So watch yourselves" (Luke 17:1-3).

## Choosing an Intentional, Shared Life

They say that Jesus rarely traveled more than thirty miles from where he was born. Some of us travel farther than that each day just to get to work. The organic kinship or "household" structures that were once the context for most people's lives have largely vanished, having been replaced in our society by rugged individualism and the dominance of multinational corporations. And yet, committed, accountable and interdependent relationships are the enduring context where transformation takes place. The mobility and resulting fragmentation in our society requires us to become more conscious and intentional about sharing life together in the kingdom of love.

At the risk of being nostalgic, I often think of the contrast between the social reality of my life and the context in which my grandfather was raised on the prairies of South Dakota. He attended a one-room schoolhouse with the children of other farming families, and after Sunday chores many of them would gather in the school building for church, singing hymns, praying and listening to the words of Scripture together. When the passage "love your neighbor as yourself" was read, it was clear who your neighbors were—the people sitting in the pews next to you, many of whom worked in the fields beside you or were related to you by blood.

For most of us, our circumstances are quite different from what was common a hundred years ago. We live away from the families and clans we were born into. Many of us work in one place, live in another and seek friendships and spiritual support elsewhere. And we don't live in a culture where the enduring paths for spiritual formation are widely known or practiced. To practice the way of Jesus we have to be intentional about how we "create" culture, reconnecting the broken pieces of a broken social reality. And we have to be more explicit in our contracts of accountability and support than perhaps previous generations did. A movement is afoot, in the church and society, to reestablish organic participatory systems where we can band together to create local communities of shared values and practices.

## Tribal Practices

*Let us not give up meeting together, as some are in the habit of doing,
but let us encourage one another—and all the more as you see the Day
approaching.*

Hebrews 10:25 (NIV 1984)

*What then shall we say, brothers and sisters? When you come together,
each of you has a hymn, or a word of instruction, a revelation, a tongue
or an interpretation. Everything must be done so that the church may be
built up.*

1 Corinthians 14:26

Making a commitment to practice the way of Jesus with six to
twelve people over a year can be a powerful step toward building
a common life. Whether you are part of a conventional church or
network of "postcongregational" companions, we can all find ways
to strengthen our life together—either through an existing group
we are part of or one that we might help start.

We call the groups we help organize tribes—and define them
as "an experimental group practice in following the way of Jesus."
Tribes are made up of people who commit to shared vows and
rhythms, practiced in community, to facilitate holistic spiritual
development. Our tribe season begins in September and concludes
in May (though people may join at any point in the year). Tribes
are led by two collaborative leaders who receive training and
coaching. Many, but not necessarily all, tribe participants have
undertaken to live by a set of vows inspired by the life and teachings of Jesus: love, obedience, prayer, simplicity, creativity, service
and community. Our yearly rhythm rotates around paying attention to the core themes from the life and teachings of Jesus described in this book (identity, purpose, security, community, and
freedom and peace).

Tribes meet weekly to remember and practice the teachings of Jesus. Each week we are either taking part in a project or learning lab or spending time together sharing a meal and the Lord's Table, praying, applying Scripture, caring for one another, and planning actions to serve and transform our neighborhoods.

In the early days of our experiments, we identified ourselves as a church community and quickly realized that using the term *church* to describe what we were doing only confused people who expected a meeting with group singing and a speaker or Bible study—something very different than what we hoped to offer. We realized that to do something new we had to shift our language and renegotiate the typical contracts between leaders and participants. So although we think a tribe is a basic form of church, we don't necessarily call it that. Describing our communities as experiments helps us remember that we haven't arrived, and acknowledges that we are in the process of learning to become communities that practice the way of Jesus together.

Each year we do a learning lab called Creating Community in which we experiment with how to practice the various belonging instructions of Jesus included in this chapter. We create quick experiments based around questions like, Who do I need to forgive? How can I stop judging? Have I been dealing directly with people who have offended me? What would it look like for us to wash each other's feet today?

We also spend time working on skills for gathering as a community in the name of Jesus. Christ-centered community can take many forms, but there are a few practices that seem to be essential to sharing life together: "They devoted themselves to the apostles' teaching and to the fellowship, to the breaking of bread and to prayer. . . . All the believers were together and had everything in common. Selling their possessions and goods, they gave to anyone as he had need" (Acts 2:42, 44-45 NIV 1984).

The earliest disciples of Jesus kept the teaching of Jesus alive, were committed to one another and met in each other's homes, shared meals and observed the Lord's Table, prayed together and pooled resources to meet needs. These tasks were the work of the people, who met in gatherings where everyone could contribute. Over time, many of these practices were ritualized and gradually institutionalized, becoming the work of professionals—though this doesn't imply that they have to remain that way.

For our Creating Community experiment, we spend six weeks cultivating a few basic practices of a Christ-conscious community. In pairs we take turns preparing community meals, offering the Lord's Table, leading a Midrash, facilitating group prayer and sharing resources.

*Preparing a community meal.* Cooking and eating together are essential expressions of belonging. Some of us may be especially gifted at this, but we are all invited to learn to practice hospitality. Here are a few basic tips we suggest for how to shop and prepare a hospitality meal for twelve to fifteen people. We like to keep these meals simple, economical (one to three dollars per person) and nutritious, with a balance of proteins, carbohydrates, vegetables and fats. We also recommend being generous with portion estimates—too much is always better than not enough—and to think through serving logistics like meal timing, utensils and cleanup. Whenever possible we try to make our meals earth friendly (local and organic and often vegetarian), using recyclable or reusable serving utensils.

*Offering the Lord's Table.* Celebrating the Lord's Table doesn't have to be a prolonged or particularly solemn ceremony.* It can be done at the beginning or end of a meal and combined with giving thanks for the food. When we practice the Lord's Table we acknowledge that we are gathered in the name of Jesus, remind-

---

*I realize that in some traditions Holy Communion is seen as a sacrament that only ordained leaders are allowed to administer. We encourage people to participate in less formal celebrations of the Lord's Table at their own discretion.

ing each other that Jesus is the source of our life together. Here's a simple pattern we encourage people to follow when they lead the Lord's Table. First, call attention to what the bread and wine represent, sharing a short reflection on the sacrifice of Jesus. Second, offer a prayer of thanks. Then, give clear directions for how the bread and wine will be distributed. We've found intinction (dipping the bread in the cup and passing it to one another) to be a very simple and efficient method. In addition, introduce a blessing for people to share with one another as the bread and wine are passed. For example, "You are the beloved" or, "This is the body and blood of Jesus given for you." Finally, it's great to end on a celebrative note. After everyone has received the elements, lift the cup and offer a toast: "To the One who has brought us into the kingdom of love, and makes us a family!" We like to make this observance part of the love feast rather than a separate ritual.

*Leading a Midrash.* *Midrash* is a Jewish term that describes a group method for investigating the Scriptures similar to *lectio divina* (divine reading). Think of the two disciples on the road to Emmaus, where Christ met them in their impassioned conversation with one another. Our goal for using this method is to wrestle with a portion of Scripture and push each other to consider how to respond with an experiment or practice. This is an activity that is best facilitated by a team of two people collaborating together.

Leading a Midrash involves a few simple steps. First, do your homework and become familiar with the text's content, themes and history of interpretation. Second, have someone in the group read the text—clearly and with confidence. Offer a brief reflection on the text and introduce a couple of provocative questions to help the group explore its meaning and contemporary relevance. Then, invite everyone to reflect on where the themes of the text intersect with their lives and how the Spirit might be speaking. To conclude, ask the group, "What is something we can ex-

periment with together between now and the next time we meet
to live into this reality?"

*Facilitating group prayer.* We take turns leading creative prayer
times using the Lord's Prayer as an inspiration. Sean and Amanda
brought a roll of paper and felt-tip pens and asked us to write or
draw what we need for our daily bread. After ten minutes, we
were invited to step back and look at what everyone else had
prayed in words and pictures. When it was Kara and Mike's turn
to facilitate they invited us to find a partner and, while seated
face to face, pray through the themes of the Lord's Prayer for the
other person (see exercise from pages 68-69). Sometimes we sit in
stillness together for fifteen minutes or invite someone into the
middle of the circle to lay hands on them to pray for healing or
blessing. It all depends on who is leading and what the needs of
the group are.

*Sharing resources.* Pooling money to distribute is a great way to
build a deeper sense of community and shared purpose. In our
tribes we invite each other to commit to giving away at least 10
percent of our incomes—5 percent to a common fund and 5 percent to the charities or institutions of our choice. We decide together what to do with the money we have collected in a common
fund according to guidelines that include prayer, discussion and
voting on spending proposals. We use a portion of the funds for
community life—to pay for things like leadership training, retreats, larger group events and celebrations. We use another portion to provide care to community members and friends—such as
when someone becomes unemployed, gets robbed, has an accident,
or needs counseling or other assistance they can't afford. We use
another portion to fund shalom-seeking projects. These might include paying for the expenses of a local community service initia-
tive (like Barrio Libre), funding travel expenses to send a group to
serve in a developing country, or donating money to agencies we
volunteer with locally.

## Seeking Peace

*If it is possible, as far as it depends on you, live at peace with everyone.*
Romans 12:18

Elaine arrived early for our tribe gathering and asked if she could speak with me privately. She seemed distraught and hesitantly began telling me how I had hurt her. We had been working on a project together in which she had volunteered to plan out the details. But when she presented her ideas I quickly glossed over them, substituting my own. She said, "I felt like you dismissed my work—and it made me wonder, do you really want my input or are you just going to do it your way no matter what?" By that time, Elaine was in tears and visibly nervous about how I might react. I told her that I hadn't been aware of what I'd done. Already feeling insecure about my role as a leader, it was painful to admit, but I had been wrong. She quickly agreed to forgive me.

Elaine's confrontation helped me recognize that I have a hard time trusting other people. For Elaine, talking to me about her frustrations was a big step toward becoming more assertive. In the past she would have quietly seethed with resentment or simply withdrawn. As we processed the tension between us, Elaine said, "I've never confronted anyone like that before." When I asked what gave her the courage this time she said, "Oh, I have to do this at work all the time. You're just the first Christian I've worked with that felt safe to confront."

Elaine's final comment haunted me, making me wonder whether the kind of "Christian" community that so many of us want eludes us because we are afraid of conflict—avoiding or denying it at all costs. The kind of belonging and transformation that is promised through practicing the way of Jesus requires us to be vulnerable with each other and to work through the difficulties that result from having our brokenness exposed.

Let's be honest—conflict is an inevitable part of any human relationship. When my brokenness rubs up against your brokenness, misunderstandings develop, feelings get hurt, expectations are unmet, and we feel disrespected or slighted. We often have a tendency to react to one another out of our insecurities and fears, or project the wounds we've received from others. And some people are just hard for us to like. We have disagreements with others because we see things from such different perspectives. And sometimes we do things, whether intentionally or not, that are plainly hurtful and wrong. We break promises and confidences. We make mistakes. We get angry and say things we regret. The question isn't "Will there be conflict?" but "How we will handle conflict when it arises?" Will we get angry? Retaliate? Become defensive? Ask others to take up our offense? Or seek restoration and forgiveness?

One day, my wife, Lisa, came home visibly shaken, with tears rolling down her cheeks. She had been with her friends Dawn and Stacey. Dawn told them that her husband had recently become so angry that he threw her across the room—and it hadn't been the first time. I too was saddened by this news, and even more concerned because Dawn's husband, Troy, was one of my closest friends. If they were having these kinds of problems, I thought, surely Troy would tell me. The next week when I went out for lunch with Troy and Stacey's husband, Matt, I tried to steer the subject of conversation toward marriage, hoping that Troy would tell us about what was going on between him and Dawn. Toward the end of lunch, I awkwardly told Troy what Lisa had told me. "Is it true?" I asked. Troy turned red and his eyes widened as he said, "I think the real issue here is why your wife has been telling you what my wife told her in confidence about our personal problems. That happened months ago. I've apologized and we've dealt with it. I don't think it's any of your business." I tried to explain that I was only trying to help—and that I assumed he would tell Matt and me about such a serious matter. "Then why did you wait almost a week to bring this up to me—and in a public place? Mark, you've really put my trust in our relationship in jeopardy today," he said. Our lunch ended abruptly in chilling silence. With my stomach in knots, I felt like I might lose a longtime friend.

I tried to call Troy several times that afternoon to see if we could come to a better understanding. In the meantime I began to wonder about my motives and what the right thing to do was in this situation. Had I brought up the issue with Troy out of concern for his marriage or because I felt hurt that he hadn't trusted me with his secret? Why had I waited to bring this up until Matt was there instead of just calling Troy immediately? Are there certain situations, like the issue of someone's safety, when it's okay to break confidences?

Troy finally called me back later that evening and we spent a long time trying to negotiate some common ground. "Mark," he said, "you've really caught me off-guard. I'm going through a lot right now and the last thing I need is to have the people closest to me ganging up on me. That's what this has felt like. I didn't tell you because it's an embarrassing issue I thought Dawn and I could handle on our own." I apologized for not being more tactful and direct, but added that I considered the matter serious enough to risk offending him. "I want you to know that I still value and respect you as a friend," I added. Troy softened, "I'll be honest, having kids and starting my new job have been incredibly stressful. It's brought up a level of anger inside me that I wasn't aware of—which, unfortunately, I took out on Dawn." Troy told me they were seeing a marriage counselor, and that he and Dawn valued our friendship. "We're here for you," I said. By the time we got off the phone, both of us were crying, grateful that we had been able to take a step to work through our conflict.

The next evening all six of us met together. Dawn and Troy told Matt, Stacey, Lisa and me more about the challenges they were facing as a couple. We also talked through the tensions that had developed between all of us. In retrospect, Dawn and Troy realized they hadn't come to an agreement about who to include in their circle of trust. Lisa admitted it would have been better if she had gotten permission from Dawn before sharing confidential information with me. I admitted that if I could do it over again, I would have spoken to Troy more privately. Even though the process was messy, it widened Troy and Dawn's circle of support and brought us all to a deeper level of intimacy and trust as friends.

Jesus dares us to imagine that we can learn to handle the challenges of our relationships in new ways. Though I'll admit, it's much easier to embrace "love your neighbor" as a lofty platitude than as a practical mandate. The situations we actually face are often confusing: You are misrepresented or treated unfairly; you have to be in a room with someone who molested you as a child; a romantic relationship ends and you're left feeling hurt; a person you tried to help takes advantage of you; or every week when you drop off the kids you have to face the spouse who mistreated you and try to forgive them again. There is no perfect way to deal with these difficulties, but we can be committed to exploring how the reality of the kingdom of love can bring us into deeper belonging. Real community happens with people who know us too well, who, despite all they know and the ways we disappoint them, still see our dignity and keep believing that we are being transformed by love.

## Discussion

- *Belonging.* Describe what your life in community has been like. What are some ways you wish you were more reconciled and better connected with others?

- *The teachings of Jesus.* Which of Jesus' instructions about community (see pages 152-53) speaks the most to you right now? How do you want the power of forgiveness and love to transform your relationships?

- *Judas.* It was one of Jesus' closest friends, Judas, who betrayed him in the end. How do you feel challenged to love the people closest to you?

- *An intentional, shared life.* How has the fragmentation in our society affected your relationships? Where do you see evidence of people reestablishing deeper kinship networks? Which of your relationships would you describe as committed, accountable and interdependent?

- *The community meal.* How important do you think hospitality is to the life of a Christ-conscious community? Describe a particularly memorable experience of sharing food or celebrating the Lord's Table.

- *Sharing resources.* Why do you think money is so often such a "charged" topic in communities of faith? How do you feel about giving money to a common fund? Brainstorm some healthy and creative ways to pool resources to meet needs.

- *Seeking peace.* How have you experienced conflict with someone? Do you have a story about working through steps of forgiveness and reconciliation? Where do you feel most challenged to live in peace and love unconditionally?

## Exercises

- *Observe the Lord's Table together as a group,* remembering that the sacrifice of Jesus shows us what love is and makes us a family.

- *Wash each other's feet.* This can be an awkward but meaningful practice that reminds us of the posture we can have toward one another. Since most of us now wear shoes, footwashing isn't the same act of servanthood in our time. Brainstorm and experiment with what might be a modern equivalent to the humility that Jesus demonstrated by washing his disciples' feet.

## Seven-Day Experiments

- *Forgive.* Are you are carrying resentments toward anyone? Begin working through steps of forgiveness this week.

- *Seek reconciliation.* Is there anyone you have potentially wronged that you are not reconciled with? Go to that person this week to seek reconciliation by admitting your faults and asking for forgiveness.

- *Admonish.* Is there someone who has wronged you who would be helped by having you approach them about it privately? Set up a time to meet with them this week.

- *Connect.* Pair up and commit to calling each other each day this week as a gesture of connection and belonging.

- *Pay attention.* Jesus once said, "Whoever welcomes [a little] child in my name welcomes me" (Matthew 18:4). Go out of your way to acknowledge the presence of children or volunteer to spend time with a child close to you.

## Extended Projects and Practices

- *Creating community.* Organize a group to experiment with the core practices of a Christ-conscious community described in this chapter: a shared meal, the Lord's Table, Midrash, prayer and pooling of resources.

- *A shared life.* Make a six- to twelve-month commitment to meet weekly as a group to practice the way of Jesus together. Set some goals about the kinds of experiments and practices you want to explore together, define your shared values and commitments, and agree on how you will spend your time when you meet.

- *Group listening and discernment.* When someone in your circle of relationship is facing a major decision about career, marriage, education or where to live, volunteer to organize and host a listening and discernment meeting. Begin with prayer. Have the person share for fifteen minutes about the factors that they are weighing. Allow some time for participants to ask clarifying questions, then discuss the group's concerns or impressions about the situation. The goal is not to tell the person what decision to make, but to collectively listen to what the Spirit might be saying, helping the person get clarity about the decision they are making. If the people in the circle will be affected by the change, involving them in this process can make transitions much easier.

# 11

# Experiments in Freedom and Peace

*Spirit of the Creator*
*We surrender*
*to the reign of love*
*In every currency of being*
*Body, mind, feelings, time,*
*In purpose, possessions and belonging*
*Make us alive to the power*
*That is making all things new.*

Mark Scandrette, 2009

Cities like San Francisco, where I live, seem to attract people who wish to reinvent themselves. I've seen a downtown corporate professional reinvent herself as a massage therapist and natural healer. I watched my thirty-eight-year-old neighbor, a skater covered in tattoos, morph into a successful businessman and real estate tycoon. I saw a shy young woman from small-town America transform herself into an arts scene diva—in only six months! We are enthralled and inspired by the possibilities of reinvention. But quitting a job, getting a haircut or buying new clothes is the easiest part. What is more challenging is learning to become a new person from the inside out—discovering new motivations, breaking old habits and finding a source of energy and love greater than our own.

Sporting a scruffy beard and old torn sweater, Brian had an intensity and honesty that were almost too much to bear. One night during our community meal and discussion, he blurted out, "I know we all want to change the world, but man, I'm so f—ed up that I can't even change myself." In a provocative way, Brian described the tension that many of us feel. The struggle to see the kingdom of God "on earth as it is in heaven" begins with a personal battle. There are forces at work in the world and within us that seek to sabotage the generative work of the Spirit. One of the reasons Jesus became such a popular teacher among the poor and discontent of his day is that he awakened their hope that a new way is possible. Yet even his earliest disciples were prone to give in to their temptations and sorrows. At the most crucial moment of his life, as he contemplated his impending death, he turned to his closest companions and found them sleeping, prompting him to exclaim, "Couldn't you . . . keep watch with me for one hour? Watch and pray so that you will not fall into temptation. The Spirit is willing, but the flesh is weak" (Matthew 26:40-41). An apprentice of Jesus learns to practice self-denial and endure the difficulties that come from living in a divided world.

## The Wilderness and the Cross: How Jesus Modeled Freedom and Peace

The temptations and sufferings of Jesus provide us with a compelling picture of the freedom and peace that we were created for. At the beginning of his public life Jesus went into the wilderness and faced three great temptations: physical comfort, material power and public reputation. Hungry from fasting for forty days, he was invited to satisfy his bodily desires, but resisted with a statement that our deepest needs are not physical but spiritual. Having the

splendor of material power paraded in front of him, he was invited
to compromise his allegiance to the invisible kingdom, but countered by affirming the supremacy of God's reign. Finally his identity as God's beloved was called into question, but he answered
with a statement that what the Creator speaks about a person cannot to be challenged. Jesus also "learned obedience through what
he suffered"—mocking, torture and abandonment (Hebrews
5:8)—and found peace amidst the excruciating pain of a prolonged execution. He invites us to deny ourselves and pick up our
crosses to discover the same freedom over temptation and peace
in suffering.

## A Vision for Achieving Freedom and Peace

What can we do about our temptations and suffering? Be awake to
God's presence and power here with us. You and I have the strength
to overcome any obstacle. We don't have to be dominated by feelings or impulses or the tyranny of rules and regulations. When we
are weary, tired, sad or discouraged we don't have to be defeated
by our addictions or compulsions. We can overcome any temptation and endure any difficulty. Grace meets you and me in the moments of our greatest weakness. We can have peace in suffering.
Nothing can separate us from the eternal source of love. This is why
we are invited to live and pray the words: "Lead us not into temptation, but deliver us from the evil one."

## What Jesus Instructs Us to Be and Do in Order to Achieve Freedom and Peace

- *Practice self-denial and embrace suffering:* "Whoever wants to be
  my disciple must deny themselves and take up their cross and
  follow me. For whoever wants to save their life will lose it, but
  whoever loses their life for me and for the gospel will save it"
  (Mark 8:34-36).

- *Deal seriously and directly with destructive habits:* "If your hand
  or your foot causes you to stumble, cut it off and throw it away.

It is better for you to enter life maimed or crippled than to have two hands or two feet and be thrown into eternal fire" (Matthew 18:6-9).

- *Abstain discretely:* "When you fast, put oil on your head and wash your face, so that it will not be obvious to others that you are fasting" (Matthew 6:16-18).

- *Perceive the difference between heart renovation and fruitless asceticism:* "Don't you see that nothing that enters you from the outside can defile you? For it doesn't go into your heart but into your stomach, and then out of your body. . . . What comes out of you is what defiles you. For from within, out of your hearts, come evil thoughts, sexual immorality, theft, murder, adultery, greed, malice, deceit, lewdness, envy, slander, arrogance and folly. All these evils come from inside and defile you" (Mark 7:18-23).

- *Avoid hypocrisy by putting the teaching into practice:* "Be on your guard against the yeast of the Pharisees, which is hypocrisy" (Luke 12:1).

- *Pray for deliverance from temptations and suffering:* "This, then, is how you should pray: . . . 'lead us not into temptation, but deliver us from the evil one'" (Matthew 6:9, 13). "Watch and pray so that you will not fall into temptation" (Mark 14:38).

- *Pay careful attention to how you see and perceive:* "Your eye is the lamp of your body. When your eyes are healthy, your whole body also is full of light. . . . See to it, then, that the light within you is not darkness" (Luke 11:34-35).

- *Be watchful, prepared and alert:* "Be careful, or your hearts will be weighed down with dissipation, drunkenness and the anxieties of life" (Luke 21:34).

- *Choose the lonely way to life:* "Enter through the narrow gate. For wide is the gate and broad is the road that leads to destruction" (Matthew 7:13). "Be perfect, therefore, as your heavenly Father is perfect" (Matthew 5:48).

## Experiments in Truth

*No discipline seems pleasant at the time, but painful. Later on, however,*
*it produces a harvest of righteousness and peace for those who have been*
*trained by it. Therefore, strengthen your feeble arms and weak knees.*
*"Make level paths for your feet," so that the lame may not be disabled,*
*but rather healed.*

Hebrews 12:11-13

David sat at the table with his head down, telling his small group
that he had gone on yet another drunken weekend bender: "I feel
like I've been struggling with the same issues for so long—I can't
tell if I'm making any progress." The "accountability" David got
from his group focused primarily on his mistakes and failures. But
being aware of our problems and confessing our missteps can only
take us so far. To really get momentum we need support and a
plan for what we can do to pursue life in the kingdom of love.
Transformation requires intentional new choices that translate
our vision and ambitions into bodily actions. This is a spiritual
secret that has largely been lost in recent times.

We all have things in our lives we wish to change. The solidarity of a group experiment can provide the resolve to make the
changes we haven't been able to make on our own. Several years
ago we began a series of shared practices to address the disparity
we often feel between how we want to live and how we actually
live. Through a learning lab we call Experiments in Truth, we invite one other to make simple but dramatic changes to our normal
habits over forty days. Out of all the experiments we've done, participants say this is the one that has brought about the most transformation in their lives.

The first session begins with a provocative question: "What is
one thing you could do over the next forty days that could change
your life forever?" Each person, through a careful process of dis-

cernment, identifies an area where change is needed and then commits to a dramatic shift—something they will stop and something they will start to address this area of concern. After we've committed to our experiments, we meet once a week to check in on our progress. Here are three examples of personal experiments in truth.

**Kyle.** As a young professional, Kyle was used to working hard and playing hard. Part of his office culture was going out after work for a late dinner and drinks nearly every night of the week. Over time this habit made Kyle feel unfocused, distracted from God and guilty about how much he regularly overspent on entertainment. For his forty-day experiment he decided to abstain from drinking alcohol or dining out and vowed to go to bed every night at a specific time. Over time, Kyle realized that the absence of alcohol made it easier for him to pray, and the money he saved by not eating out allowed him to give a full 10 percent of his income away—and he generally felt more freedom and peace.

**Brandon and Rebecca.** Over the years that Brandon and Rebecca had been married they struggled to make physical intimacy and time together a priority. Their needs for emotional support and sexual closeness often went unsatisfied. They decided that for their forty-day experiment they would commit to having sex at least three times a week. What they discovered was that pursuing more regular sexual intimacy required them to communicate better, which had positive effects in many other areas of their relationship as well. By the end of the forty days they were experiencing more unity, romance, trust and fun than at any other time during their seven years together.

**Rachel.** Rachel recognized that she masked a deep sense of insecurity through an obsession with fashion, shopping and meticulous grooming. For her experiment she made a vow not to shop or wear jewelry or makeup for six weeks. Shifting her attention away from her appearance and clothes helped her focus on developing peace and inner beauty. People immediately began to notice a dramatic change in her disposition and affirmed her natural radiance. (Note: Other participants have struggled with the opposite issue, a lack of self-care, and have experimented with giving more attention to their physical appearance.)

The first step to designing an Experiment in Truth is to *examine your life.* Spend some time in solitude asking God to reveal where transformation is most needed. In what area do you long for healing and greater wholeness? Do you have any longstanding habits or thought patterns you would like to see change? What are the daily choices that distract you from loving God and people? For some of us, self-reflection can feel like an unwelcome reminder of guilt or shame. If the voice you hear is more condemning than inviting, then it's probably not the authentic voice of the Spirit. Remember that it's God's kindness that leads us to repentance (Romans 2:4). The Greek term for repentance suggests "to think differently after, to have a change of mind and heart." In contemporary vernacular we might say "rethink," "reimagine" or "dare to dream up your whole life again."

Our lives are shaped by the choices we make about where we spend our basic life energies. Some questions to consider: How do I live in my body? What do I think about or dwell on in my mind? How am I managing my feelings and the stresses of life? Where am I spending my time, talents and resources? How am I showing up to my relationships? After reflecting on where you spend your life energy, you can determine one or two priority areas where changes are most needed.

A second step is to *explore the pattern and root causes* for the issues you've identified. On a piece of paper, briefly describe the issue or pattern. What are the daily choices you make that support this habit or pattern? Are there deeper issues from which this struggle arises? How does the way of Jesus speak to these conditions?

Several years ago I invited a group of trusted friends to speak into my life through a feedback process described later in this chapter. When I asked, "What are my blind spots?" more than one friend told me that they didn't feel entirely safe around me because of how critically I spoke about other people. One person wrote, "It makes me wonder what you say about me when I'm not in the room." It was painful to hear, but they were right. As I prayed and thought more deeply I came to realize that my tendency to criticize stemmed from insecurities about my own identity, which made me jealous of other people and their accomplishments. To make myself feel better, I would focus on their weaknesses or flaws. For my Experiment in Truth, I resolved not to say anything negative or critical about anyone for forty days. I also committed to write a letter each day to affirm and encourage someone that I had been jealous or critical of. Over the course of the experiment the whole posture of my relationships began to shift. A year later, one of the friends who had confronted me, not knowing about my experiment, spontaneously said, "I notice that you don't talk badly about people anymore."

A third step is to *decide what new practices to adopt* in order to address the issues you've identified. If we want to change, we have to risk new ways of being and doing. It might help to ask, If I change what I do in my mind and body (e.g., what I eat, how I spend my time, what media I consume, how I use my money and who I spend my time with), how will it affect my capacity to flow with the Creator's energy and love? Consider including a physical change like exercise or avoiding junk food, and a mental discipline like keeping a gratefulness journal or abstaining from social-networking websites. Sometimes it works to replace an old practice with a new practice that is incompatible with the old (e.g., replacing smoking with exercise). An effective experiment will include both elements of abstinence and engagement—something you will stop doing and something you will start doing as a healthy alternative.

Heather told her small group that she struggled with being worried and anxious. "I know this might sound funny or freakish," she said, "but when I'm feeling anxious I clean my house compulsively. When I'm feeling really overwhelmed, I will clean for three or four hours a day! I suppose it helps me feel like I have more control. I also try to escape bad feelings by watching TV until late at night—and then I don't get enough sleep." Heather wanted to feel more peace and less anxiety. For her forty-day experiment she decided to stop watching television and limited herself to cleaning for only thirty minutes a day. She also decided to start keeping a prayer journal and committed to getting at least eight hours of sleep each night.

One of the reasons we call these "experiments" is that we are testing what changes actually make a positive difference. The goal is never to create an extra layer of rules that we use to judge ourselves or others by. People sometimes confuse an Experiment in Truth with the dietary restrictions commonly associated with Lent. For most of us our deepest need for change won't be addressed by eating fish instead of meat or giving up chocolate until Easter. We need practices of abstinence and engagement that are specific to the places where reinvention is most needed in our lives.

One of the common mistakes people make is choosing an experiment that is vague or difficult to measure. "I'm going to try to walk more" doesn't have the teeth to motivate like "I am going to walk two miles at 7:00 a.m. every Monday through Friday for the next six weeks." A good experiment is specific, measurable and realistic, and includes asking when, where, and how often it will be performed. It's important to have a place where you track and record your daily progress, like a spreadsheet. An experiment that requires intensity and daily consistency will yield better results than one that is occasional or sporadic. Try to pick changes that are realistic and attainable but also challenging and substantive. Even if the prospect of making a permanent change seems too daunting, most people find a forty-day commitment achievable—especially when done in solidarity with a supportive group.

Once you've identified what to start and what to stop, a fourth step is to *commit to your plan*. This is where the ancient wisdom of vows is instructive. I might want to love God and people and feel a strong desire to do so, but without a commitment to specific practices these are just sentiments. A vow or promise translates my good sentiment into tangible actions: "For you, God, have heard my vows; you have given me the heritage of those who fear your name. . . . Then I will ever sing in praise of your name and fulfill my vows day after day" (Psalm 61:5, 8). We show what we really believe and value by what we are committed to actually do. With Experiments in Truth we invite each other to make written commitments that are signed by at least one other person that we are accountable to each day. We also share our plan with a small group of people that we check in with each week. If one of our practices seems too personal or potentially embarrassing to discuss, we share it with at least one person and refer to it as our "private" experiment at group check-ins.

At the first check-in meeting after we began our personal experiments, Megan sheepishly said, "I'm finding out that I'm not very good at doing anything that requires discipline or self-control." It can take time to discover just how much vigilance and effort are required to enact changes to longstanding patterns. Your body may be conditioned to expect certain comforts or stress relief, and when denied them will show resistance to change. Committing to new limits can reveal a degree of compulsivity you weren't aware of or the fact that you aren't quite ready or willing to change.

The first time Eric participated in Experiments in Truth, he decided to work on his complacency: "I don't push myself—so I rarely get around to doing healthy things like regular exercise. And I often feel overwhelmed by pressures at work and wonder if daily prayer might help." He made a commitment to get up every day by six-thirty to pray, and to exercise three times a week. At the end of forty days Eric couldn't tell if the practices had made any difference. He hadn't kept consistent records, but estimated that he had prayed one or two days a week and exercised once a week. Realizing that half-trying hadn't worked, the next year Eric chose to address the same issues, but with much greater intensity and resolve. He decided to pray as he walked to work each day (instead of taking the bus) and committed to going to the gym five times a week. This time Eric was able to be consistent and at the end of forty days he was ecstatic about the results: "I feel much more centered and physically healthy." Recently Eric reported that he has now maintained his new rhythms for over a year, and added, "Now that I've proved I can do it, I think I'm ready to tackle a much bigger issue—facing my fears."

A final step is to *evaluate your experiment* after you've completed it. Were you consistent in following what you set out to do? Did the new action, pattern or discipline you chose create the results and momentum you hoped for? How would you like to make this new practice part of your ongoing rhythm of life? At the end of our experiments we also ask each other, "What advice would you give to someone trying the Experiment in Truth for the first time?" Here's a list of top recommendations:

- Don't skip a single day. When you allow yourself to skip just once it makes it easier to lose track of the whole experiment. But if you do miss a few days, don't give up—keep trying.

- Avoid all-or-nothing thinking. Don't get hung up on having to do it exactly as you planned, but pay attention to refining the experiment as you go.

- Check in daily with a partner and carefully track your progress.

- Think through how you can discretely explain your new choices to people who become curious.

- It's difficult to do an effective experiment when your life is in transition or crisis.

- Be aware that your experiments may expose a wound you didn't know you had.

- Focus on the process rather than results, and remember that your experiment is a spiritual discipline and not just an exercise in willpower.

## Personal Growth Feedback

*Be diligent in these matters; give yourself wholly to them, so that everyone may see your progress.*

1 Timothy 4:15

Through Experiments in Truth we encourage each other to listen to the voice of the Spirit, read the circumstances of our lives and receive wise insight from advisers. Sometimes we need help from others to distinguish between the authentic whisper of the Spirit, the phantom echoes of our culture and what I call the "monkey voices" in our heads—those compulsive or negative thoughts that replay in the brain. Trusted friends and wise counselors can help us see the blind spots that sabotage our growth and recognize the progress we can't see on our own. During Experiments in Truth we each send personal growth feedback surveys to between five and seven people we trust to help us identify strength and growth areas and get discernment about any life decisions or transitions we may be facing. Then we process the feedback responses we get together in small groups.

The first step to gathering feedback is to *brainstorm your circle of support,* which might include a parent, siblings, your spouse or children, friends or housemates, coworkers and mentors. They should be people who know you well, are aware of your blind spots and can speak to your dignity. Be sure they are people who are safe for you that can be trusted to give constructive feedback. But still consider including voices who might not tell you what you want to hear. Ideally they will be people who have made a significant investment in your life or have a stake in your future.

A second step is to *consider how to communicate with your circle of trust*. What is the best way to get the feedback you are requesting? Sending an email message with the questions attached will be fine in most cases. Your circle of trust will need several weeks of advance notice to thoughtfully fill out the survey and get back to you by your deadline. You might consider contacting respondents who are less comfortable with technology by mail or telephone. If you use the phone make sure that you take careful notes. In most cases, you will get more thoughtful and honest feedback through written responses than by a voice-to-voice conversation. With the amount of correspondence and scheduling that many people have, don't be surprised if you have to send three separate messages to get back a completed survey. It might help to contact the people in your circle of trust with a friendly reminder and thanks every other week up until your feedback deadline.

With anticipation and a bit of trepidation, Emily sent out personal growth feedback surveys to both of her parents, a sister and several good friends. It felt extremely vulnerable to ask for their input, and she was afraid that what they said might be harsh or overly critical. She trembled a bit as she typed out the last note:

Dear Mom,

I'm participating in a workshop called Experiments in Truth, a 40-day spiritual exercise that includes getting feedback and input from trusted friends and mentors. A premise of this course is that one of the ways the Spirit speaks is through the wisdom and council of those we know. That's why I'm contacting you. I am going through a process of discerning my personal strengths and growth areas. And I'm seeking wisdom and clarity about an important life decision.

As a trusted voice in my life, I would like to invite you into this process. Would you be willing to respond to the following questions and send them to me by Monday, March 22nd? Please don't hesitate to share your most honest thoughts that can help me grow as a person.

Thanks in advance for your thoughtful response!

*Affirm my strengths and potential:*

- How have you experienced me and in what contexts have you seen me most empowered and alive?
- What do you see as my strengths and gifts?
- What do you think I was made to do? Where do you see me in 5, 10 or 15 years?
- What is my best contribution to the world? How do I best serve those around me? Where do you sense God at work in my life?

*Help me become more aware of my growth areas:*

- What are my blind spots? Are there any areas in my life where you sense a lack of self-awareness or sensitivity to others? Are there unhelpful ways that I affect the people around me that I might not be aware of?
- How do I generally come off to people? Are there positive or negative comments that people make after being with me that would be constructive for me to be aware of?
- Where do you sense a need for greater wholeness, growth or maturity in my life?

*Share your wisdom and insight:*

- What cautions, concerns or advice would you give me at this stage in my life?

- Right now I am trying to gain clarity on the following life decision: *I'm weighing whether to move back home to Washington to finish up a degree in library science, or stay in San Francisco and try to finish up my degree here. If I move back to Washington where I have residency, I can begin studying right away and can get financial aid. If I stay in San Francisco, I will have to go to school an additional year because of credits that won't transfer and, due to living costs, will probably have to take out a large loan.*

- The questions I am asking about this decision are: *Is library science a good fit for me? Is moving away to finish school worth leaving my community in San Francisco, which has become like a second family to me?*

A third step is to *process the responses you receive and develop appropriate action steps.* Each person Emily contacted took her request very seriously and spent a lot of time forming their responses. Some of the things they shared were predictable and a few were painful but true. Her small group listened to Emily reflect on the feedback she received and helped her distinguish between impressions that were accurate and well informed and those that seemed to express the peculiar biases of a single respondent. Many of the people Emily contacted offered good counsel about the decision she faced about whether to relocate for school. But what surprised her most was the overwhelming encouragement and affirmation she received. Several people told her she had a lot of wisdom and insight to share and pushed her to be less tentative and more confident in her leadership. Emily had a tendency to gloss over the positive affirmation she received and focus on any negative comments. Her small group encouraged her to find ways to remember and celebrate the affirmations she received as well as developing action steps to address her growth edges. The most memorable feedback came from a whimsical friend who, referencing Winnie the Pooh, wrote, "I think you would do well to put some Tigger in your Piglet," encouraging her to be more daring and bold.

There is an inevitable gap between how we see ourselves, how others see us, and who we really are. We can choose to dismiss the feedback we receive, be devastated by critique or embrace our vulnerability with a sense of invitation to follow the caring voice of the Spirit into greater possibilities. When Jesus first approached the disciple Peter, he replied, "Go away from me, Lord; I am a sinful man" (Luke 5:8). Jesus helped Peter realize there was more to his life than the limits and brokenness that he was so painfully aware of. We practice the way of Jesus by facing who we really are—and from there, find a source of courage, hope and momentum to take our next steps into the kingdom of love.

## Discussion

- *The teachings of Jesus.* Which of the statements Jesus made about freedom from temptation and peace in suffering (see pages 170-71) do you find most compelling? Why? Where would you like to experience more success over temptation and peace in suffering?

- *Reinvention.* Can people change? If so, how do people change? Explain.

- *Cooperation.* How would you describe the dynamic between the power of your choices and the activity of God's Spirit within you?

- *Experiments in truth.* What immediately comes to mind when you read this question: "What is one thing you could do over the next forty days that could change your life forever?"

- *Root causes.* Reflect on the potential patterns or root causes contributing to the behaviors you struggle with. How have you dealt with patterns of temptation and brokenness in the past? What has been most helpful?

- *Vows and promises.* Describe a time you made a vow. What were the benefits you experienced? Do you feel hesitant or empowered by the thought of making explicit promises? Why?

- *Personal growth feedback.* Reflect on a time you invited someone to speak wisdom or guidance into your life. How was it helpful? Do you find it more difficult to receive praise or criticism?

## Exercise

- As a whole group or in triads, *respond to these questions:*
  - What are the things that keep me from living more fully into God's dream for my life?
  - Where inside do I sense a battle between the work of the Spirit and the vulnerabilities of mind and body?
  - Jesus invites us to pray, "Lead us not into temptation, but deliver us from the evil one." Lay hands on one another and pray for God's freedom and peace to come to the struggles that have been shared.

## Seven-Day Experiments

- *Decide on a shared discipline of abstinence,* something that you will commit to stop doing for the week. A media fast is often a discipline of abstinence that many people can relate to.

- *Each night for seven nights spend a few minutes before bed reflecting on your day using these questions* (often called the prayer of examen):
  - When was I aware of God's presence or love?

- When did I feel alone, weary or tired?
- Where do I hear the invitation to enter the rest of apprenticeship to Jesus more fully?
- *Decide on a shared discipline of engagement,* something healthy that you will commit to doing for the week. Meditating on a portion of Scripture or fixed-hour prayer might be activities that most everyone can relate to.

## Extended Projects and Practices

- *Experiments in truth.* Organize a group of friends to do a forty-day experiment like the one described in this chapter.

- *Personal feedback inventory.* Either as part of your work in experiments in truth or as a separate activity, select a group of people to fill out personal feedback inventories for you. Process the responses you get and decide how you will act on the feedback you receive. Sample questions that can be modified to your situation are included in the appendix.

- *Mentor.* Identify a mentor who you will meet with four to six times a year to talk through your personal growth goals. Or commit to meeting weekly with a small group of peer mentors who can provide more intimate support and accountability.

- *Rule of life.* Identify your life goals and priorities, and brainstorm the daily, weekly and seasonal habits or practices you need to cultivate in order to keep momentum (examples: Sabbath keeping, service, physical labor, spiritual friendship, silence and solitude, travel, sabbatical, exercise, sleep, study, time in nature, family rhythms, etc.).

# Conclusion

Risk Being Fully Alive

A man once began a very long journey. Along the road, he stumbled upon a bag of gold. The bag was heavy, but he hoisted it up over his shoulder and continued to walk. Down the road he went, hunched over with the bag of gold over his shoulder, leaning to one side.

Walking past a town, he saw a beautiful young woman seated on a rounded stone. They talked and his heart skipped a beat, though she soon turned away. The stone she had sat upon reminded him of her beauty and his longing, and so he decided to take it with him. Bending forward with his arm outstretched, he began to roll the stone. Down the road he went, hunched over with the bag of gold over one shoulder, stooping to roll the stone with his other arm, and working up a furious sweat in the noonday sun.

At a desolate place along the road, he saw a pig wander past, oinking. *I should like to own a pig and eat its tasty bits,* he thought to himself. Since there was no one around to claim the pig, he caught it with a rope and tried to lead it down the road. But the pig was too slow. So he tied the other end of the rope to his own ankle and dragged the pig behind him. Down the road he went, hunched over with the bag of gold over one shoulder, stooping to roll the stone with his other arm and dragging the pig behind.

Walking past a field he saw a blackberry bush. Because he was hungry he stopped to eat, greedily picking and eating the blackberries while scratching his face and hands on their thorns. Soon his teeth and mouth were stained purple by the fruit's sweet juice and his hands became sticky and dark. Down the road he went, hunched over with the bag of gold over one shoulder, stooping to roll the stone with his other arm and dragging the pig behind, with his face and hands scratched and stained with sweet, sticky blackberry juice.

The man continued to travel for many days, only stopping to pick more blackberries or to rest in the shadows. One hot night he stopped to sleep but awoke to discover that all he had carried had been stolen—the gold, the stone and the pig! At daybreak he dusted himself off and continued on his way, now empty handed and free of his burdens. But by force of habit, he continued to walk as if he still carried the bag of gold, the rolling stone and the pig on a rope. Down the road he went, hunched over, stooping with his arm extended and dragging a foot behind, his face and hands still scratched and stained by the sweet, sticky blackberry juice.

A young boy watched as the man limped past, mesmerized by his peculiar appearance. The boy turned to his grandmother, standing nearby, and asked, "What makes this man look so strange, and why does he walk so funny?"

Looking up as the man passed by, the grandmother replied, "The road is straight, but the man is crooked, made that way by all he tried to carry and the hunger he could never satisfy. One day you, too, my child, will take on the shape of your journey, by what you wish for and what you carry."

✦   ✦   ✦

Each of our lives is made up of what we have wished for and what we have carried. The invitation of the Master is to leave behind what can only make us weary and tired to enter the Sabbath rest of the kingdom of love. We begin like the man, who, though free of his burdens, continues on with a limp and a stoop, scratched and stained. It's time to wish for what only love can bring, to be cleansed and healed and to stretch out our limbs to walk in new ways.

We have been invited into a life together in the kingdom of love, to discover our identity as the Father's beloved, to enact our purpose as agents of the Creator's healing purpose, to find our security in the abundance God provides, to embrace community through a source of love that is greater than our own, and to experience a freedom and peace beyond the limits of our strength or understanding. We enter by the sacrifice of the One who is the Way, and we learn to walk by practicing his Way.

What does it mean to follow the way of Jesus in our time? And where will our experiments take us? The goal of shared practices is to become fully alive to the power that is making all things new. We act from the belief that we are on a pilgrimage that will last through our final breaths. In the spiritual realm as in the scientific, experiments lead to more questions that beget further experiments, just as reaching the top of one vista reveals the path upward toward another, more beautiful view further up and farther in.

I long to see the church of Jesus Christ manifesting the love that we were made to give and receive. I dream of a time when groups in every community become centers that practice and teach the Way, training people to do everything that Jesus did and taught. I'm convinced that modest, incremental changes to "normal" Christianity or "church as usual" will not get us where we need to go. As leaders, dreamers and visionaries we need to lead not just by what we say, but by how we subversively live out the alternatives. Many in our generation have been free to critique what is, but few of us have had the courage to enact the changes we can imagine. Some of us need to step out and humbly risk more radical steps of obedience. As Wendell Berry memorably said, "If change is to come . . . it will have to come from the margins. . . . It was the desert, not the temple, that gave us the prophets."* What seems dangerous, heretical or impossible today might not seem so tomorrow.

So much of our lives is designed around minimizing risks, avoiding pain and managing the chaos and uncertainties that are inherent to the human condition. We are tempted to look to governments, corporations or social structures (including religion) to give us the certainty and security we crave. Yet the One in whom we live warns us that it is foolish to live cautiously (Matthew 25:14-30) and calls us away from the safety and conventions of our kingdoms into the mystery and adventure of the kingdom of love. Those who inherit this kingdom do so with reckless abandon, not looking back, and betting it all on the pearl of greater price, to risk being fully alive.

Where will practicing the way of Jesus take us? To the place where it has always taken disciples since the beginning, toward the fault line of love in our time: to suffering, persecution, misunderstanding and death, this is where his footsteps lead, and to peace and hope beyond the struggles of this age. The greater question is not whether we are willing to suffer, but will we risk being fully alive?

A friend recently reminded me that I once joked that if I was ever asked to write a book it would be called *Make Your Own D\*\*\* Life*. When you opened the cover, all the pages would be blank. It would have been much easier to write than the book you are now reading (and it may have sold more copies too!). Alas, the sentiment remains. I hope what has been written here inspires you to embark on your own adventures that might fill books with stories

---

*Wendell Berry, *The Unsettling of America* (San Francisco: Sierra Club Books, 1977), p. 174.

about your journey to practice the way of Jesus and make a life together in the kingdom of love.

The inevitable question is, where to begin? All you have to do, and all you can do, is take your next step . . . and when you do, please share what you discover by posting your stories and reflections at www.jesusdojo.com.

## Discussion

- *What you wish for and carry.* What struck you about the parable of the man on the road ? How would you relate this story to the role of experiments and intentional shared practices?

- *Life in the kingdom of God.* What captivates you the most about the invitation to live in the kingdom of love?

- *Risking radical obedience.* What do you think a person has to risk to be fully alive to God's kingdom? What are some historical consequences for those who have chosen to follow the way of Jesus?

## Exercises

- *First steps.* What do you feel like the Spirit is inviting you to do in response to the material explored in this book? What is the most daring thing you can imagine doing?

- *Levels and kinds.* Remember the three levels of experiments that you can be involved in: person centered, group initiated and open invitation. Who can you imagine taking risks of obedience with in each of these levels?

- *Group journey.* How might your group or church community incorporate experiments and shared practices into your life together? Try to think in terms of one-time, short-term and long-term experiments or practices.

- *Identity.* What are your next steps to embrace your identity as

God's beloved. What are some shared experiments or practices you would like to try?

- *Purpose.* What are your next steps to enacting your purpose as an agent of God's healing? What are some shared experiments or practices you would like to try?

- *Security.* What are your next steps to finding your security in God's generosity and abundance? What are some shared experiments or practices you would like to try?

- *Community.* What are your next steps to living in reconciled relationships and Christ-conscious community? What are some shared experiments or practices you would like to try?

- *Freedom and peace.* What are your next steps to experiencing greater freedom and peace? What are some shared experiments or practices you would like to try?

# Study Guide

$W$hat follows is a six-session study guide for exploring the material in this book in a group setting. Each session includes suggested chapter readings from parts one and two of the book, discussion questions and seven-day experiment ideas to choose from. (Every practice and experiment included in this guide has been done by one of our communities in the Bay Area.)

Groups should select a seven-day practice to experiment with each session; longer-term experiments are included for groups that intend to journey farther together. Visit www.jesusdojo.com for more group resources and additional study guide materials.

## SESSION 1: AN INVITATION TO EXPERIMENT / EXPERIMENTS IN SECURITY

- Read chapters one and nine prior to the session.
- Select discussion questions from pages 24-25 and 146-47.
- Choose and commit to a seven-day experiment in security from chapter nine.

## SESSION 2: FOLLOWING THE WAY OF THE RABBI / EXPERIMENTS IN IDENTITY

- Read chapters two and seven prior to the session.
- Check in with one another on the seven-day experiment in se-

curity you committed to as a group in the previous session.

- Select questions to discuss from pages 38-39 and 120.

- Choose and commit to a seven-day shared experiment in prayer from chapter seven.

### SESSION 3: CREATING SPACE FOR SHARED PRACTICES / EXPERIMENTS IN COMMUNITY

- Read chapters three and ten prior to the session.

- Check in with one another on the seven-day experiment in prayer you committed to as a group.

- Select questions to discuss from pages 53-54 and 164-65.

- Choose and commit to a seven-day shared experiment in community from chapter ten.

### SESSION 4: THE VISION AND PHYSICALITY OF SPIRITUAL FORMATION / EXPERIMENTS IN FREEDOM AND PEACE

- Read chapters four and eleven prior to the session.

- Check in with one another on the seven-day experiment in community you committed to as a group.

- Select questions to discuss from pages 67-68 and 183-84.

- Choose and commit to a seven-day shared experiment in freedom and peace from chapter eleven.

### SESSION 5: HOW PRACTICE CHANGES US / EXPERIMENTS IN PURPOSE

- Read chapters five and eight prior to the session.

- Check in with one another on the seven-day experiment in freedom and peace you committed to as a group.

- Select questions to discuss from pages 82-83 and 136.

- Choose and commit to a seven-day shared experiment in purpose from chapter eight.

## SESSION 6: INITIATING AND LEADING GROUP EXPERIMENTS / CONCLUSION

- Read chapter six and the conclusion prior to the session.
- Check in with one another on the seven-day experiment in purpose you committed to as a group.
- Select questions to discuss from pages 98-99 and 190.
- Develop your next steps using the questions at the end of the conclusion.

# Appendixes

# Discerning Your Life Purpose

- *What am I passionate about? When do I feel most alive, vital and energized?* Your answer to these questions can help you identify the unique way that you were made to be of use in this world.

- *How would I describe my personality and temperament? Am I an introvert or extrovert? What core yearnings motivate my actions and decisions?* When you are reflecting on your vision and goals, it is important to consider the gifts and limits of your personality. You don't have to become someone else. Imagine scenarios that are realistic to who you were created to be.

- *Who is calling out the best in me? What do people recognize and affirm about my best contribution to the world?* The feedback you receive from people who know you well can provide important clues about your destiny.

- *In what areas do I long for greater wholeness in my personal life?* Each of us has wounds or struggles that we must face and surrender as we enter God's light more fully. Part of your journey as a person is discovering healing and finding ways to manage your weaknesses.

- *Where do I sense the greatest need for justice and healing in our world?* The needs of suffering people in our world (both local and worldwide) can seem overwhelming. No one person can hold all that pain and struggle. Each of us has been given sensitivity to a certain frequency of needs. What is breaking your heart that breaks the heart of God? Is it the physical needs of those in poverty, the emotional needs of those who are displaced, lonely or abused, or something else?

- *Who are the people in my life that are important for me to care for and journey with over my lifetime?* This question acknowledges the fact that we are not meant to live as isolated individuals. Who are the stakeholders in your life (e.g., family, friends, a particular place and people)?

- *What are my strongest talents, passions and skills? Where can they be of greatest service to others?* You've been given skills, talents and expertise that can be leveraged for the good of the world. One of our primary life tasks is discerning how to best utilize these resources.

- *How does the work I presently do contribute to the greater wholeness that God desires for all of humanity?* It can help to make a connection between what you are already skilled to do with how you hope to contribute in the future.

- *As you have worked through this survey, what are two or three "ahas" that can help you get clarity on your particular path for enacting your purpose as an agent of God's healing?*

# Gratitude and Contentment Survey

With an awareness of global economics in mind, rate God's provision and your satisfaction in the following categories.

---

**FOOD**

| Lacking | Basic/Adequate | Abundant | Luxurious |
|---------|----------------|----------|-----------|

Satisfaction: YES/NO

---

**CLOTHING**

| Lacking | Basic/Adequate | Abundant | Luxurious |
|---------|----------------|----------|-----------|

Satisfaction: YES/NO

---

**SHELTER**

| Lacking | Basic/Adequate | Abundant | Luxurious |
|---------|----------------|----------|-----------|

Satisfaction: YES/NO

---

**SAFETY**

| Lacking | Basic/Adequate | Abundant | Luxurious |
|---------|----------------|----------|-----------|

Satisfaction: YES/NO

---

**RELATIONSHIPS**

Lacking    Basic/Adequate    Abundant    Luxurious

Satisfaction: YES/NO

**HEALTH CARE**

Lacking    Basic/Adequate    Abundant    Luxurious

Satisfaction: YES/NO

**TRANSPORTATION**

Lacking    Basic/Adequate    Abundant    Luxurious

Satisfaction: YES/NO

**EDUCATION**

Lacking    Basic/Adequate    Abundant    Luxurious

Satisfaction: YES/NO

**RECREATION**

Lacking    Basic/Adequate    Abundant    Luxurious

Satisfaction: YES/NO

If we begin with contentment for basic necessities, we can receive anything more as a special gift.

# Assets of Abundance Survey

Many of the things we enjoy most are beyond monetary value. Rate the following nonmonetary assets in terms of how much you value them.

---

**FAMILY, FRIENDS AND COMPANIONS**

Low value      1            2            3            4            5        High value

---

**SPIRITUAL CENTEREDNESS**

Low value      1            2            3            4            5        High value

---

**CREATIVE EXPRESSION**

Low value      1            2            3            4            5        High value

---

**NOBLE, USEFUL WORK OR SERVICE**

Low value      1            2            3            4            5        High value

---

**FREE TIME, PHYSICAL ACTIVITY**

Low value      1            2            3            4            5        High value

---

**THE PLEASURE OF ENJOYING FOOD**

Low value      1            2            3            4            5        High value

**LISTENING TO MUSIC**

Low value 1 2 3 4 5 High value

**ENJOYMENT OF ARTS, CULTURE, KNOWLEDGE**

Low value 1 2 3 4 5 High value

**MARRIAGE, ROMANCE, SEXUAL PLEASURE**

Low value 1 2 3 4 5 High value

**SABBATH REST**

Low value 1 2 3 4 5 High value

**RELATIONAL INTIMACY**

Low value 1 2 3 4 5 High value

**EMOTIONAL HEALTH, STABILITY**

Low value 1 2 3 4 5 High value

**FREEDOM, LIBERTY**

Low value 1 2 3 4 5 High value

**OPPORTUNITIES TO LOVE AND SERVE**

Low value 1 2 3 4 5 High value

**ACCESS TO INFORMATION AND LEARNING**

Low value 1 2 3 4 5 High value

**REALIZED SKILLS AND TALENTS**

Low value 1 2 3 4 5 High value

**ACCESS TO NATURE AND CULTURE**

Low value     1          2          3          4          5     High value

**PHYSICAL SAFETY**

Low value     1          2          3          4          5     High value

**A SENSE OF SECURITY AND PEACE**

Low value     1          2          3          4          5     High value

**PHYSICAL HEALTH**

Low value     1          2          3          4          5     High value

**CHARACTER AND WISDOM**

Low value     1          2          3          4          5     High value

**PATIENCE AND JOY**

Low value     1          2          3          4          5     High value

**FORTITUDE TO ENDURE SUFFERING, GRIEF, LOSS**

Low value     1          2          3          4          5     High value

**THE BEAUTY OF THE NATURAL WORLD**

Low value     1          2          3          4          5     High value

**(OTHER)** _____

Low value     1          2          3          4          5     High value

- What did you realize about what you value during this exercise?

- How much are these assets of abundance worth in comparison with all of your material possessions and financial assets?

- Why do you think we tend to overvalue material possessions and undervalue God's assets of abundance?

# Learning Lab Invitations

**AWAKENING CREATIVITY**
Exploring the hidden story of your life
Dates: April 5-May 10, 7:00-9:00 p.m.
Final public performance/art event: Friday, May 14, 7:00-10:00 p.m.
Cost: $60-$150 sliding scale (includes curriculum, art materials, facility use and final reception costs). Scholarships available upon request.

Do you aspire to be more creative? Since ancient times spiritual seekers have expressed their questions and longings through poetry, art and song. Jesus invited his listeners to repent, reimagine or dream up their whole lives again. Many have observed the vital link between imagination, creativity and spiritual transformation. This six-week learning lab will help participants integrate creativity, personal narrative and theology through individual and group exercises. A final group show featuring the work of participants will occur on Friday, May 14, from 7:00 to 10:00 p.m.

Participants will

- learn to use daily journal keeping, a weekly walk and creative adventure as tools for transformation

- study the life and teachings of Christ as an archetype for creative living

- explore personal narrative through artistic media (including poetry, dance, prose, music, sculpture, photography, drawing and painting)

- discuss process and discoveries through small group encounter
- create a compilation of art pieces from weekly exercises for display at a group show

✦ ✦ ✦

## EXPERIMENTS IN TRUTH

A laboratory for personal transformation
Dates: Tuesdays, February 24-April 7, 7:00-9:00 p.m.
Cost: $60-$100 sliding scale

The Master invites us to rethink (or reimagine) our whole lives in light of the Maker's dream of greater wholeness for our world. This learning lab explores the physicality of spiritual formation. How will changing what I do in my mind and body (what I eat, how I spend my time, the media I consume, how I use my money, who I spend my time with) affect my capacity to flow with the Creator's energy and love? This practical workshop seeks to deal with the disparity we often feel between how we want to live and how we actually live.

Jesus spent forty days in the wilderness fasting and facing his greatest temptations. Participants in this learning lab will engage in practices aimed at confronting our own shadows and obstacles to the spiritual life through "experiments in truth," including

- a forty-day experiment applying disciplines of abstinence and engagement to personal growth issues

- a greater cognitive understanding of the holistic nature and physicality of spiritual formation

- a practical experience of group discernment that helps you listen to your life, hear the voice of the Spirit and receive the wis-

dom and insight of friends to help you have greater clarity about
your decisions

- the development of a comprehensive personal growth plan to
  help you maintain longer-term momentum and consistency
- time with an identified mentor who will help you work through
  your growth plan, teach you a skill, or share wisdom and insight

# Contracts of Participation

**AWAKENING CREATIVITY**

I understand that by participating in Awakening Creativity I am committing myself to an intensive process of discovery and transformation that will require a significant investment of my time over the next six weeks.

- I commit myself to participate in all learning lab meetings.

- I will do daily journal-keeping, homework exercises, the weekly walk and creative adventure, and create pieces for the final show.

- I will share authentically with my small group and listen gently and respectfully to others, keeping appropriate confidentiality.

- I understand that participation in this lab will require an hour of my time each day.

- In order to maximize my experience, for the duration of this learning lab I commit myself to excellent self-care, good eating, exercise and sleep habits, and careful planning of my schedule.

Signature: _____

Date: _____

✦  ✦  ✦

## ABOLITION PROJECT

I understand that I am committing to a six-week intensive formation exercise that will require

- participation in six weekly project gatherings
- 2-4 hours of weekly homework exercises and research
- personal vulnerability and self-examination
- changes to my normal pattern of eating and purchasing
- a sliding scale donation for supplies and facility costs
- collaboration on a group project
- additional shared expenses for some group projects

I will

- arrive on time to weekly project meetings
- contact the organizers if I have to be absent
- be responsible, ethical and compassionate with the information I obtain on human trafficking
- do nothing that would endanger victims of human trafficking
- not share names of suspected businesses or publicize mapping information outside of appropriate sources
- be generous and humble with people who may be less informed than me about this issue
- be respectful, sensitive and caring in my interactions in the neighborhoods where we meet—treating the people on the street with dignity

Signature: _____

Date: _____

# Personal Feedback Inventory Sample Letter

Dear _____,

I'm participating in a workshop called Experiments in Truth, a forty-day spiritual exercise that includes getting feedback and input from trusted friends and mentors. A premise of this course is that one of the ways the Spirit speaks is through the wisdom and counsel of those we know. That's why I'm contacting you. I am going through a process of discerning my personal strengths and growth areas, and am seeking wisdom and clarity on some life decisions.

As a trusted voice in my life, I would like to invite you into this process. Would you be willing to respond to the following questions and send them to me by [fill in date]?

Please don't hesitate to share your most honest feedback that may help me clarify my strengths and growth areas. I will be reviewing the responses I receive as a step in developing a personal growth plan.

Thanks in advance for your thoughtful and honest response!

## AFFIRM MY STRENGTHS AND POTENTIAL

- In what contexts have you seen me most empowered and alive?
- What do you see as my strengths and gifts?
- What do you think I was made to do?

- Where do you see me in five, ten or fifteen years?

- Where do you sense God at work in my life?

- What is my best contribution to the world?

- How do I best serve those around me?

### HELP ME BECOME MORE AWARE OF MY GROWTH AREAS

- What are my blind spots?

- Are there any areas where you sense that I lack self-awareness or sensitivity to others? Are there unhelpful ways that I affect the people around me that I might not be aware of?

- How do I generally come off to people? What impressions do people have of me? Are there positive or negative comments that people make after being with me that would be constructive for me to be aware of?

- Where do you sense a need for greater wholeness, growth or maturity in my life?

### SHARE YOUR WISDOM AND INSIGHT

Right now I am trying to gain clarity on the following life decision: [fill in description]

The questions I am asking about this issue are: [list your questions here]

- What cautions, concerns or advice would you share with me at this time in my life?

- Knowing the kind of person that I am, what other insights would you share with me about this issue?

# Experiments in Truth Evaluation

1. Briefly describe the facets of your forty-day experiment—the issues you sought to address and the disciplines of abstinence and engagement you committed to.

2. What did you learn through your experiment?

3. Which aspects of your experiment proved to be the most transformational?

4. What do you want to carry from your experiment into your everyday life?

5. If you were to do an exercise like this again, what would you do differently?

6. What would you recommend to someone else embarking on a forty-day life transformation experiment like this?

Please rate (circle) your experience of the following (N/A = did not complete).

---

**PERSONAL REFLECTION EXERCISES:**

| Amazing | Helpful | Not Helpful | N/A |

---

**IDENTIFYING A MENTOR:**

| Amazing | Helpful | Not Helpful | N/A |

**FEEDBACK LETTER EXERCISE:**

Amazing              Helpful              Not Helpful              N/A

**GROUP DISCERNMENT PROCESS:**

Amazing              Helpful              Not Helpful              N/A

**PERSONAL GROWTH PLAN:**

Amazing              Helpful              Not Helpful              N/A

Describe your experience with the weekly learning lab sessions.

**SMALL GROUP DISCUSSION:**

Amazing              Helpful              Not Helpful              N/A

**WHO WAS YOUR GROUP FACILITATOR?** _____

How would you rate their facilitation skills?

Excellent            Good                 Fair                     Lacking

What helpful feedback or suggestions would you give this person?

**ORIENTATION AND COACHING:**

Amazing              Helpful              Not Helpful              N/A

What helpful feedback or suggestions would you give the facilitators?

Was there anything about Experiments in Truth that seemed awkward or confusing? Explain.

How could we improve the experience of this learning lab?

Would you recommend this learning lab to a friend?   YES   NO

**THANKS FOR YOUR FEEDBACK!**

# The Vows of
# ReIMAGINE Tribes

*To Creator, obedience*
*To Creation, service*
*To each other, community*
    *In all things, love, in all things, love*
*With possessions, simplicity*
*For life, prayer*
*In our world, creativity*
    *In all things, love, in all things, love*

A vow is a solemn promise made before God and people to take or refrain from a specific action. A vow expresses sentiment, intention and a commitment to specific practices.

> For you have heard my vows, O God;
>     you have given me the heritage of those who fear your
>         name. . . .
> Then will I ever sing praise to your name
>     and fulfill my vows day after day. (Psalm 61:5, 8 NIV)

When a group of people makes promises together they are able to support and encourage one another in their resolutions. We see making common vows as an earnest attempt to obey Jesus in the details and direction of our daily lives. Our specific commitments, practices and rhythms are continually evolving because we see each year as a new phase of this experiment. Below is a summary of our current commitments to God and one another:

*1. Obedience.* We recognize Jesus as our teacher and authority, and we wrestle with how to surrender to the way of love in every detail of our lives. We submit ourselves to one another in love, and we strive to keep our vows to God and our commitments to one another.

- We are obedient to the Ten Commandments and the law of love.

- We meet with a trusted mentor or peer-mentor to talk about personal growth at least six times a year (a personal growth plan should be written on your own or with your mentor).

- We seek community discernment on major life decisions (change of vocation, marriage, relocation, personal crisis, etc.) through listening meetings.

*2. Service.* We are made to collaborate with our Maker in caring for all of creation. We recognize the sacredness of work, and we use the capacities of our minds and bodies to serve others with our talents and skills according to the needs of the place where we find ourselves.

- We give priority in our schedules to serving one another and, as our season of life allows, the forgotten and marginalized.

- We do our work with dignity, to provide income and fulfill our true vocation, in ways that promote equality, sustainability and justice in our world (directly and indirectly).

*3. Community.* We seek to practice forgiveness and reconciliation, honor, encouragement, humility and hospitality in all of our relationships. We are committed to taking the journey of faith in solidarity with our sisters and brothers around the world.

- We are active in projects and family meetings.

- We participate in all tribe gatherings.

- We practice regular hospitality by welcoming people into our homes, lives and events.

**4. Simplicity.** We acknowledge the abundant provision of our Maker and seek to live in trust, radical contentment and generosity within an empire of scarcity and greed.

- We live by a budget that reflects sustainability and intentional conscientious priorities. We share these budgets in a yearly members meeting.

- We give away at least 10 percent of our income (5 percent to our common work and 5 percent to the charities of our choice).

- We collectively take an annual inventory of our belongings and evaluate what to keep, share, sell or give away.

- We live by a schedule that allows for our mental, physical, spiritual and emotional selves to be replenished and available (weekly Sabbath, room for spontaneity, pace of life, conscientious commitments, etc.).

**5. Prayer.** We seek the fruitfulness and guidance of the Spirit that comes from being centered and surrendered to the will and presence of our Creator. We practice rhythms of prayer, study, silence and solitude that help us remain open to the voice and power of the Spirit.

- We create space in our schedules to pray twice a day.

- We take an annual two-day silent, contemplative prayer retreat.

- We participate in common prayer once a week.

**6. Creativity.** We seek to be awakened in our imaginations and actions, inspired by the epic story of God's kingdom and creation, and connected to our cultural context. We want to live artfully, taking risks, experimenting, and using the language and media of our culture to explore the unfolding story of God's kingdom together.

- We cultivate divine imagination by reading the Scriptures daily within our family or household.

- We seek to find God through intentional and reflective interactions with nature and culture.

- We create cultural artifacts (recipes, poems, paintings, songs, stories, etc.) and share them with each other each year, recognizing their importance as signposts of our journey.

- We practice body and mind disciplines (exercise, sleep, healthy eating, rest, etc.) that promote health and sustainability.

7. *Love.* We acknowledge that love is the greatest force in the universe, and in every dimension of our lives we seek to cooperate with the reign of God's love.

- We actively seek to meet one another's needs.

- We seek reconciliation in all relationships, past and present.

- We seek unity, cooperation and goodwill with groups and individuals seeking God in the way of Jesus, both locally and globally.

# Credits and Thanks

Thank you to the cast of characters who helped design or facilitate the shared experiments and practices included in this book: Nate Millheim, Sean Blomquist, Mike McCoy, Adam Klein, Damon Snyder, Amy Ross, Sarah Montoya, Jeff and Melissa Hinn, Rev. Shinko Rick Slone, Melanie Hopson, Darian Ahler, Melody and Derek Hansen, Charley Scandlyn, Michael Toy, Dave Maddalena, Tom and Elaine Bible, Cody Birkey, Dani Scoville, Lauren Crandall, Nicole Myers, Laura and Daniel Kirk, and Chris King.

Many of the seeds for these experiments and shared practices were planted through early "think tank" sessions with Dallas Willard and the cofounders of ReIMAGINE, Dr. Linda Bergquist, Dieter Zander and Rod Washington.

Thanks to everyone who allowed their stories of struggle and transformation to be shared in these pages.

During the writing process I was encouraged and instructed by the stories of friends and communities who have sought to apply the perspective and practices described in this book to a variety of contexts: Nate Millheim with Shalom in Oakland, California; Chris and Christine Kernaghan with Campus Crusade for Christ in San Francisco; Dixon Kinser at St. Bartholomew's Episcopal in Nashville, Tennessee; Sean Randall, Ryan Walton, and Keith and Char Klassen in Sacramento; David Sunde at Riverbend Church in Austin, Texas; Stian B. Kilde Aarebrot at Sub Church in Oslo, Norway; Tony Kriz in Portland, Oregon; Alex Schweng at Grace Church, Fremont, California; Charley Scandlyn at Menlo Park Presbyterian in Menlo Park, California; Richard Lundblad in Santa Rosa, California; Mark Biebuyck at Kensington Church, Troy, Michigan; and Chad Whitehead and company at Mount Olympus Presbyterian in Salt Lake City. Thanks also to the many student groups and churches who have participated in our "Jesus Dojo" intensives in San Francisco over the years.

A dedicated group of early readers, from a wide variety of backgrounds, provided helpful feedback on an early version of the manuscript. Thanks to Stian B. Kilde Aarebrot, Luis Fernando Batista, Elaine Bible, Steffen Boeskov, Jonathan Brink, David Cobia, Dr. Todd Harrington, Chris Kernaghan, Keith Klassen, Tobias Kron, Richard Lundblad, Paul Lai, Craig Nason, Jarrod Shappell, Alex Schweng, Cam Sobalvarro, Mike Stavlund, David Sunde, Ryan Walton and Betsy Wang. Special thanks to Dr. Gary Black, Darren Prince and Keoke King, who provided detailed textual comments.

I'm grateful for my editor, Dave Zimmerman, and Andrew Bronson and the marketing team at IVP, and for my agent, Greg Daniels. You've made the development of this book a gratifying process. Grateful acknowledgment to Sheryl Fullerton, who believed I had something to say and cultivated my voice as a writer. And thanks to *Conspire* magazine for providing an early outlet for some of these ideas.

And finally, thanks to Lisa, Hailey, Noah and Isaiah, the four people with whom I've shared the most intimate and amazing shared formation experience—being a family.

# About the Author

Mark Scandrette is the founding director of ReIMAG-INE, a center for life integration in San Francisco. A sought-after voice for creative, radical and embodied Christian practice, he leads retreats and workshops, mentors pastors and leaders, and provides spiritual direction. He lives with his wife, Lisa, and their three children in an old Victorian in San Francisco's Mission District. He is also the author of *Soul Graffiti* (Jossey-Bass).

For booking information and inquiries visit

www.markscandrette.com

## About ReIMAGINE

ReIMAGINE is a center for life integration based in San Francisco. The mission of ReIMAGINE is to help people be revolutionized by the life and teachings of Jesus and to empower leaders who can revolutionize their communities. Our dream is to see leaders and communities of practice cultivated and supported across the United States and around the world. We pursue this dream by communicating a vision for life together in the kingdom of love, inviting participants into transformational group experiments and developing leaders who can teach and lead others. For more information visit

www.reimagine.org

## Also by Mark Scandrette

*Free: Spending Your Time and Money on What Matters Most*

For more information visit www.ivpress.com

formatio

TRADITION. EXPERIENCE.
TRANSFORMATION.

Formatio books from InterVarsity Press follow the rich tradition of the church in the journey of spiritual formation. These books are not merely about being informed, but about being transformed by Christ and conformed to his image. Formatio stands in InterVarsity Press's evangelical publishing tradition by integrating God's Word with spiritual practice and by prompting readers to move from inward change to outward witness. InterVarsity Press uses the chambered nautilus for Formatio, a symbol of spiritual formation because of its continual spiral journey outward as it moves from its center. We believe that each of us is made with a deep desire to be in God's presence. Formatio books help us to fulfill our deepest desires and to become our true selves in light of God's grace.